C++ for dinosaurs

Guide for readable, maintainable, reusable and faster code

Nick Economidis

C++ for dinosaurs

Guide for readable, maintainable, reusable and faster code

Nick Economidis

This book is for sale at http://leanpub.com/cpp_for_dinosaurs

This version was published on 2014-07-30

ISBN 978-1-312-36766-1

©2014 Nick Economidis

Contents

Preface i
    Who is this book for i
    How to read this book ii
    Why this book was written ii
    Acknowledgements: iii

Discussion 1

1 Understanding why a style change is needed 3
    1.1 Elements of wasteful programming style 3
    1.2 Why is C++ a better choice than C for most cases ? 8
    1.3 Why people don't switch to C++ ? 9
    1.4 Object oriented approach critique 11

2 Steps for embracing a better coding style 13
    2.1 Step 1: Use readable syntax for function arguments 13
    2.2 Step 2: Use the STL containers 16
    2.3 Step 3: Do not write raw for-loops 18
    2.4 Step 4: Algorithms should read like pseudocode 26
    2.5 Step 5: Make use of the roll/unroll behaviour 28
    2.6 Step 6: Revamp your callback methods 32

3 Efficiency advantages using STL and C++ 39
    3.1 Templates are faster than macros 39
    3.2 Efficiency of std::string vs char* 42
    3.3 Order of complexity does not reflect performance 43
    3.4 Old speed issues that don't exist anymore 44
    3.5 map vs unordered_map 47

4 Am I doing it right ? 49
    4.1 bind-mania 49
    4.2 loving low-level data structures 56
    4.3 for_each everywhere 59
    4.4 replicating STL algorithms 61

Learning the details 65

5 Expressing intent using STL algorithms 67
- 5.1 Customising algorithms with comparators 68
- 5.2 Customising algorithms with predicates 69
- 5.3 Copying algorithms 70
- 5.4 How are algorithms implemented ? 72
- 5.5 What is the fastest way to learn STL algorithms ? 75

6 Callable Objects 77
- 6.1 Using functions as callable objects 77
- 6.2 Using function objects as callable objects 78
- 6.3 Using `std::bind()` to create callable objects 82
- 6.4 Lambda functions as callable objects 84
- 6.5 When to use each type callable functions: 85
- 6.6 `std::bind` by example 86

7 Avoid using low-level strings 93
- 7.1 Problem description 93
- 7.2 The solution 95

8 Understanding cache issues 97
- 8.1 Running costs of a program 97
- 8.2 Data access costs 98
- 8.3 Costs depending on data structures 99
- 8.4 Instruction Pipeline 99
- 8.5 Side-stories 102

9 Converting a .c module into a .cpp 105
- 9.1 Ensure header is readable by C++ 106
- 9.2 Mark external functions as extern "C" 107
- 9.3 Replace implicit casts from void * 108
- 9.4 Replace `<math.h>` with `<cmath>` 108

10 References 109

Preface

Habits are the brain's actions in power-saving mode. Experienced programmers evolve habits so that they can save energy in common tasks, and spend it in solving difficult problems.

Dinosaurs are the experienced programmers in the company who have evolved a style of programming featuring a certain pattern of habits. The older the dinosaurs are, the more obstinate they are. They aren't willing to break these habits, because they work fine for them.

From the aspect of development, this argument is actually right; development is usually faster when you use habits and don't stand to think for simple things. For the whole program though, development only accounts for about 15% of the temporal effort, while maintenance accounts for nearly 80%. There are habits, especially old ones, that have a serious impact in reading, understanding, and therefore maintaining code. This includes both other people's code, or even one's own, two-month-old code.

In this book I am addressing such habits, and provide alternative ones, based on contemporary instruments provided by C++.

This book is not about teaching for a paradigm-shift. It is about writing C++ using native idioms, not like C, Java, or Fortran.

The book makes use of features in *C++03* and *C++ Technical Report 1 libraries* (tr1). So, any compiler after 2005 should support the contents of this book. Certain features of C++11 are also discussed as an alternative, where applicable.

Who is this book for

- This book was originally aimed for *engineers* and *programmers* who strongly believe in C. Most bad habits stem from practices developed by the low-level nature of C. The problems of these habits are demonstrated and alternatives are offered. The book contains all the necessary material, so that C programmers can get the kickstart they need to embrace C++.
- *C++ programmers* will benefit from the style described in this book. Their style is often filled with impurities inherited from Java and C books.
- Students will find a guide to creating professional looking coding style. Colleges very rarely provide any incentive for writing quality code. This book bridges the gap between knowing C++ and writing good code.

If you care about software quality but fear that it takes huge organisational changes to achieve it, this book is the missing link towards your goal.

I am describing steps that you can take to write clear code. This is an important quality because:

- Clear code increases readability.
- Readable code allows your partner to have an opinion about your code.
- Readable code is the prerequisite for code reviews.
- It is other people's eyes that spot bugs, not tests[1].
- Clear code also promotes maintenance.

Prerequisite knowledge

- This book will *not* teach you C++. I expect that you can write C or C++ without much difficulty. I suppose that at least six months of working experience or a couple of years of exercises at college should be enough in order to appreciate this book.
- You do not need to know C++, but you should be able to write in C.
- *No* object oriented programming knowledge is required.

How to read this book

The first half of the book can be read sequentially. I demonstrate the characteristics of poor code that I am addressing. Then I describe the common arguments of those who resist adopting C++ and explain how I am going to invert them. Finally, I describe the six steps that you can take to write clearer code.

Throughout the first chapters, there are references to the second part of the book. All examples and demonstrations are studied in separate chapters. This gives me enough space to go into greater depths. It makes reading the whole concept smoother, too.

Why this book was written

I studied Electrical Engineering in the mid 90's, and I was taught C and Matlab for problem solving. I only used C for production code.

I have worked on programs that already had a lifetime of more than 10 years. This means that they carried a lot of legacy code. The features had to be delivered fast and there was hardly ever enough time for proper programming.

Most of my career I had to use C and C++. However, there was always an underlying rule that C was to be preferred. There was not enough trust that C++ had a significant advantage – C++ was thought

---

[1] tests are written to spot bugs that you know they exist, so that they do not appear again. But tests do not discover bugs.

of as an object-oriented language. Indeed, I have made a lot of regrettable errors in my projects, as a result of experimenting with features of C++, especially object-oriented programming. However, I always felt a strong distaste whenever I had to switch to C.

Finally after ten years, through the advancements of C++ and some experts' ideas, I feel that I can present (without remorse) some ways C programmers can use to create elegant, readable, yet traditional programs.

These ways involve the use of certain C++ features to make good old-fashioned C code read and work better. They have nothing to do with object oriented programming. It is not the most suitable solution for most problems anyway.

I presented these advancements through a series of lectures to my colleagues, and it was the first time that I managed to change the dinosaurs' attitude towards C++. In fact, they were so interested that *they* encouraged me to write this book.

In this book I will demonstrate how C-style makes code unreadable, buggy and slow. I will show the features of C++ that deter people from adopting it, and how to fix this issue. I will present a few basic rules, that will change how you write, not how you think. Ultimately, with this style shift, your code will read nicer, you will reduce the bug count, and your program may even run faster.

Acknowledgements:

This book collects the best ideas and suggestions about readable code, presented recently by Sean Parent, Bjarne Stroustup, James Coplien and Trygve Reenskaug. Their presentations were so inspiring I felt I had to test, present and write about them. This book serves as a testimonial that their proposals actually work for production code, and are also easy to learn and adhere to.

The cover of this book was painted by Chrysa Malama[2].

---

[2] http://rabbithole2014.blogspot.com/

Discussion

1 Understanding why a style change is needed

1.1 Elements of wasteful programming style

In order to appreciate where programmers' energy is wasted, I will demonstrate it on a walkthrough of a program written in a C-style. The most prevalent symptoms of wasteful coding style are:

- Readability of low-level code
- Repetition
- The fight against pointers
- Overuse of macros

1.1.1 Readability of low-level code

Imagine you need to get the *current working directory*. You search the web, and find that the library function to use is getcwd() of <direct.h>.

Now, how much effort is wasted in order to decipher how to use this function ?

```
char *getcwd (char *cwd, int sz);
```

- does *the function* allocate and return the string ? What is the cwd and sz for, then ?
- do *I* allocate the string, then pass the pointer and size to it ? What is the return value for then ?

Then you find out that you can use it like

```
char cwd [FILENAME_MAX] = "";   /* 1024 chars alloc, in <stdio.h> */
getcwd (cwd, FILENAME_MAX);
```

Passing a pointer to some pre-allocated memory makes sense,
because dynamic memory allocation is not possible on some devices. In such cases, hard-coded buffers are used for storage. C is a low level language, and this is an important factor in why this function was designed this way.

But wait, FILENAME_MAX may not be enough for UNC paths! The manual states that we have to check for correct allocation:

```c
char cwd [FILENAME_MAX] = "";
if( !getcwd (cwd, FILENAME_MAX) ) {
    if (errno == ERANGE) {
        // not enough space allocated
    } else {
        // some other error
    }
}
```

You replace the static allocation with a dynamic one, using `malloc()`:

```c
int sz = FILENAME_MAX;
char *cwd = malloc(sz);
if( !getcwd( cwd, sz ) ) {
    if (errno == ERANGE) {
        do {
            sz *= 2;
            cwd = realloc(cwd, sz);
        } while (getcwd(cwd, sz) == NULL && errno == ERANGE);
    } else {
        // some other error
    }
}

free(cwd);   // don't forget to free !!
```

Pretty complicated, but it now looks that this implementation is complete enough.

Now, you don't want to replicate this code every time, so this is an opportunity for code-reuse. You ask somebody in your team to turn this into a function and add it to your corporate library. Then you call it like:

```c
char *cwd = get_current_working_directory();

free(cwd);   // don't forget to free !!
```

Great job, +1 for corporate thinking! Run it. Later, during the day, it crashes at some weird place. Why?!?

The programmer thought it was a good idea to have a `static` string implementation, so that you do not have to call `free()` all the time.

But how are you supposed to know that without reading some documentation ? Oh well, it doesn't matter now, fix the bug by removing the call to `free()`.

```
char *cwd = get_current_working_directory();
```

Oh, and since the string pointer is now managed by the get_current_working_directory(), you shouldn't change it - make it const

```
const char *cwd = get_current_working_directory();
```

Yes, this code is clean now, and readable. Hey, didn't you hear the news ? Your fellow programmer found that instead of writing that horrible loop, he could call getcwd() like

```
const char *get_current_working_directory() {
    return getcwd(NULL, 0);
}
```

Now you have a memory leak...

> Why so much fuss for just a string ?

1.1.2 Repetition

After having a meeting and decide that you prefer the static version of the string, you start writing your actual function.

```
const char *cwd = get_current_working_directory();
if (cwd) {
    foo();
    goo(cwd);
}
```

Wait! if foo() makes a call to get_current_working_directory() then cwd will be invalidated! Better keep a temporary copy of it:

```
const char *cwd = get_current_working_directory();
if (cwd) {
    char *tmp_cwd = strdup(cwd);
    foo();
    goo(tmp_cwd);
    free(tmp_cwd);
}
```

Ok, this is safe. But notice how much noise you have added:

- `tmp_cwd` does not add to the readability
- to be safe you make copies of the string every time you use it.

1.1.3 C-style errors

In time, the code inside the braces might grow. But you always have to remember to `free` the temporary string

```
const char *cwd = get_current_working_directory();
if (cwd) {
    char *tmp_cwd = strdup(cwd);
    foo();
    goo(tmp_cwd);
    free(tmp_cwd);
}
```

However, this might get out of hand if the code has to exit the scope early:

```
const char *cwd = get_current_working_directory();
if (cwd) {
    char *tmp_cwd = strdup(cwd);
    foo();
    if (something) return;   /* leak: tmp_cwd not freed */
    goo(tmp_cwd);
    free(tmp_cwd);
}
```

All these nonsense could have been avoided if you used a C++ implementation for the `get_current_working_directory()`, using a simple `std::string`:

```
string get_current_working_directory();
```

You needn't worry about *constness*, about *copying*, about *freeing*, or *leaving out of scope*.

```
string cwd = get_current_working_directory();
if (!cwd.empty()) {
    foo();
    if (something) return;
    goo(cwd);
}
```

 std::strings were quite controversial with regard to efficiency. Read the relevant chapter, on efficiency of low level strings, compared to std::strings.

1.1.4 Overuse of macros

Macros is a primitive tool for creating template code. It uses parametric textual replacement to achieve creation of boilerplate code with small changes between its different copies.

In rare cases it is the only tool that you can use. Indeed, Boost uses it to reduce massive code duplications.

However, widespread use often leads to bugs – hard-to-detect ones. These range from the typical macro-bug patterns, to cases that slow down your program by small undetectable fractions each time.

Here are some examples:

the classic macro bug: passing an argument with side-effects

```
int i = 20;
int y = SQUARE (i++);
// what's the value of 'i' here ?
```

This buggy pattern is taught in every self-respecting seminar. When SQUARE is expanded in code will call i++ several times. Expansion usually produces code that compiles. I know of no static analysis tool that can catch that error. The only thing that you can do to spot that, is to use capital letters that shout *this is a macro, proceed with caution*.

Macros are often used because they inline code, which is thought to lead to faster execution times. However, unless macros treated specially, execution times will get slower:

arguments with no side-effect are not so harmless, either

```
char sentence[] = "a long sentence";
int y = SQUARE (strlen(sentence));
// how many times was strlen() called ?
```

Sometimes, because of this widespread belief, people use macros, without even considering calling their equivalent functions. Even worse, sometimes they don't even bother providing both the macro and function version of a routine.

when an equivalent function is not available, or it is cumbersome to call it

```
for (...) {
        QSORT ( int, array1, array1_size, COMPARE_INTS );
        QSORT ( int, array2, array2_size, COMPARE_INTS );
        n = count_common_numbers (array1, array1_size, array2, array2_size);

        QSORT ( int, array3, array3_size, COMPARE_INTS );
        QSORT ( int, array4, array4_size, COMPARE_INTS );
        m = count_common_numbers (array3, array3_size, array4, array4_size);
}
```

Such cases can easily introduce cache misses in the instruction cache. Chapter templates vs macros explains why this may happen.

Macros use a special syntax, involving #, ## and \, which may be hard to follow. Also, it is impossible to step into a macro using a debugger. The macros are expanded before the compiler kicks in. Therefore, the debugger has no knowledge of their existence.

All these issues constitute widespread usage of macros as a bad habit.

1.2 Why is C++ a better choice than C for most cases ?

C is still the language of choice for many applications, although in principle, Java and C# should be the best fit for the majority of the software that is built.

The reason for this is that native languages, in principle, run faster or use fewer power on mobile devices. C is also cross-platform. The C-standard committee treats backwards-compatibility as a feature of the language. This fact promises longevity of projects, which is also a strong economic factor for choosing this language.

Apart from the objective reasons though, C is an easy language that allows programs to be developed at a good pace, with good chances of completion. C is the language for teams that don't want to experiment with language features, but prefer to concentrate on the product.

C++ has more high level features than C. Therefore, in principle, C++ should be the choice for the most or larger projects. However, C had a mature standard during C++'s infancy. It is only after Technical Report 1 of C++ standard that the language can demonstrate its great potential. The library features introduced at that time, combined with the speed increase of those libraries, now makes C++ a better choice.

1.3 Why people don't switch to C++ ?

These are the most common punchlines by people who resist change:

- many language features encourages experimentation.
- not a single book for learning C++
- "C++ is slower"
- awful compiler errors
- too many rules - virtual functions, templates, operator overloading
- portability of older C code.

1.3.1 Many language features encourages experimentation

C++ has such a wide scope that it is a challenge to learn all of it. Some people find that scary, and they stick to the C part. Some people, on the other hand, get excited and want to experiment with everything. Experimenting on a product, just for the programmer's self-satisfaction is dangerous, and managers ban C++ to minimise this temptation. What I am proposing, instead, is to teach this part of C++ which makes the same C style code readable and maintainable. Teaching how to use C++ should reduce the experimentation and also enable everybody to write in a clearer and more familiar style.

1.3.2 There is not a single book for learning C++

You only need one or two books to learn 90% of C. Most people will agree on which these two books should be. The book count that achieves this goal for C++ is about ten to fifteen. I hope that this book will be the one that C programmers need to continue working the way they already know, only clearer.

Most books tend to use C++ as Java (everything is an object, design patterns everywhere, abstractions, UML diagrams). I think that the best style for C++ is: *object-oriented* only when necessary, and very light on *templates*. It is the style that Stroustrup demonstrates. It is also the style that is most suitable for programmers with a C background. Out of all the books I have read, *Accelerated C++* was the one that was most effective for learning.

1.3.3 "C++ is slower"

This is the favourite pun by people that resist change. And it is partly true. You can't take a C program, shove it in a C++ compiler and expect it to work as fast as it did.

However, C++ can make your programs run faster than the C programs if you follow this book's style. In fact, with less struggle, your programs will run faster because the optimiser will have more chances in kicking in, more data are likely to be in the cache. What I am saying, is that you can rest assured that your everyday C++ code will be faster than your everyday C code, and that would reduce your tendency for premature optimisation.

1.3.4 C++ has too many rules

C++ has too many rules - virtual functions, templates, operator overloading.

Many of these rules have to do with object oriented programming. Although it is powerful and systematic, object oriented programming (OOP) is the best approach for only 10% of the programs, where natural hierarchies exist in the domain. For the rest of the programs, the good-old top-down or bottom-up approach can be at least as good as any other.

Operator overloading is a feature that mainly API or library programmers might be interested in, but not for most developers. It is of minor importance, therefore I will only use the parts that are necessary for the purpose of this book.

Templates are useful in making your algorithms read like pseudo-code. I will only show you the least amount of template knowledge that can make a great difference to your code. Again, at the end of the day, it is not necessary to learn how to compose templated code, but only use it.

1.3.5 Portability of older C code.

C++ is not 100% compatible to C code. You can't just rename a .c into a .cpp and expect it to compile. But the modifications you need to do are minimal and standard. I shall demonstrate all the cases that I have experienced.

1.3.6 Awful compiler errors

This is a major drawback. Compiler errors when calling or writing template functions can be daunting. Most of the times, looking at the first, or the last line of the error will help you spot the problem. The LLVM compiler also tends to give a much better error description. There is hope that *concepts* of C++'14 will allow compilers to produce decent error messages.

Unfortunately, I can't give you solutions to this problem. But if you think about it, templates are like macros. And compiler errors produced by macros are a nuisance, too. Even so, I prefer spending my time trying to make the compiler work, rather than struggling with the debugger to catch pointer-related errors - an everyday task in C. In C++, if you adopt Stroustrup's style, you can reduce pointer-related bugs to almost zero.

1.4 Object oriented approach critique

From a C professional's point of view, the object oriented approach to solving a problem looks like it requires a major change in the way one thinks, and is too cumbersome to implement. And indeed, it is.

If you follow the guidelines of a typical book on object oriented design[1], you may easily end up with a program where it is too hard to follow its execution path. In most programs you may encounter, an algorithm is scattered into various classes[2]. There, your only hope to following the code flow is via a good debugger, not just by reading it. You will be forced to write unit tests in hope that this will catch the bugs that your eyes cannot see.

You will have to invent unthinkable names for classes, trying in vain to explain the functionality that was pushed in them. You will then have to reinvent names, as you refactor to make your design better. You will be charmed by the beauty of design patterns. You will create abstract classes and virtual functions to eliminate every other if statement, struggling to make the code more readable.

You will read and follow new methodologies - Agile, XP, Scrum - hoping to get you back to speed again, since the maintenance effort of program has climbed up and you cannot satisfy your customers like you did.

This odyssey can go on for many years. You will try every so many solutions designed around OOP, hoping to get you out of the mess that OOP has put you into in the first place. A design expert can steer you directly to the proper way looking at objects, but until then you are on your own.

On the other hand, OO approach can be a great way of looking at a problem, provided that the domain objects already express a natural hierarchy. A hierarchy that everybody recognises. But if the objects are so few, the chances are that you can already cope with this in C - using function pointers probably.

Concluding, I would say that if you do not feel that the OO approach is the natural way to solve a particular problem, then you are better off sticking to a traditional top-down or bottom-up approach.

---

[1] *James Coplien*, in *Lean Architecture*, refers to classical approaches to object oriented design as *your grandfather's object oriented design*.

[2] *Trygve Reenskaug* in his speech during Øredev provides a very nice picture of what properties good code should demonstrate. His speech is titled *"DCI: Re-thinking the foundations of object orientation and of programming"*

2 Steps for embracing a better coding style

The following guidelines can be embraced one-at-a-time. Each of them will elevate the readability of your code to the next level. They are not sorted in order of significance, but rather in an order that one can learn them.

2.1 Step 1: Use readable syntax for function arguments

The ideal function should make clear what it does just by looking at the function call. The reader should not have to jump to the function definition to find what it does. He shouldn't even have to look at the declaration.

Careful choice of a function name[1] can assist readability, but it should also be clear to the user whether the function will modify its arguments, or not.

To demonstrate this, let's consider how you would comprehend an unknown piece of code, where you know that all variables involved are int or double:

```
double a, b, c, d;
...
c = parametric_addition(a, b);        // (1)
accumulate_results(a, &b, c, &d);     // (2)
```

Reading these lines,

1. you may wonder what `parametric_addition()` does, but you have no reservations that a and b are read, and c is the result.
2. it may not be clear how `accumulate_results()` accumulates a and c to b and d, but you are sure that b and d are meant to store some result, and a and c are only read.

 This is a typical case – despite programmers' efforts for producing good function and variable names, the intent is not always obvious to the reader. But return type and the way you pass the arguments can greatly affect readability, and it can easily be standardised.

Although the above way of passing parameters is helpful, when it comes to passing large data structures, programmers diverge from it, for performance reasons.

When variables are of a large data structure, some programmers tend to pass the values *by pointer*:

---

[1]Robert C. Martin's book, *Clean Code*, contains a comprehensive chapter on how to create proper names for functions and classes.

```
LongReal a, b, c, d;    // 1Kb each
...
parametric_addition(&a, &b, &c);
accumulate_results(&a, &b, &c, &d);
```

Even worse, sometimes they pass the values *by reference*:

```
LongReal a, b, c, d;    // 1Kb each
...
parametric_addition(a, b, c);
accumulate_results(a, b, c, d);
```

Both treatments are a knock out kick for the poor reader. Even if the function names were perfect, passing values this way would simply throw away all the effort of creating a good name.

But it is possible to write like this:

```
LongReal a, b, c, d;    // 1Kb each
...
c = parametric_addition(a, b);
accumulate_results(a, &b, c, &d);
```

and still be efficient. Just follow these rules:

 Rules of thumb for function arguments:

- when an argument is meant to be **read-only**
    - pass it *by value* if it is small,
    - pass it *by const reference* if it is big.
- when an argument is meant to serve as an **input-output**, pass it by pointer.
- when you need to **output** a result, *prefer* returning it, rather than passing a pointer to it.

In other words:

read-only parameters should be passed by value, or by const-reference

```
void log (int value);                  // few bytes
void log (const LongReal &value);      // many bytes
void log (const std::string &value);   // potentially many
```

input-output parameters should be passed by pointer

```
void largest_and_smallest_values (int *smallest, int *largest);
```

output parameters should be returned, rather than passed by pointer

```
// prefer this
LongReal add_two_real_numbers (LongReal a, LongReal b);

// rather than this
void add_two_real_numbers (LongReal *result, LongReal a, LongReal b);
```

Even though returning a large value used to be expensive, compilers now make this efficient by employing *RVO optimisation*. Read chapter 3.4 on how to achieve it.

This implies that

1. you should always avoid passing by non-const reference, and
2. you should avoid allocating a value in the heap in order to return it, because `malloc` and `new` can be *unpredictably* slow, and somebody has to `delete` them.

```
// passing by reference is bad for readability
void foo (LongReal &a, LongReal &b);     // (1)

// allocating a value to return it is poor practice
LongReal* add_two_real_numbers (LongReal a, LongReal b);   // (2)
```

Stroustrup, in his book[2], describes his rules of thumb for getting the same result. Google coding standards[3] also support this way of passing parameters.

---

[2] The C++ Programming Language (C++11), 4th edition, chapter *12.2.1, Reference Arguments*, on page 318.
[3] http://google-styleguide.googlecode.com/svn/trunk/cppguide.xml

2.2 Step 2: Use the STL containers

The C++ Standard Library (STL) provides a collection of containers that

- has a homogeneous interface
- is well documented
- is well understood
- is fast and optimiser-friendly
- is type-safe
- is highly parameterisable
- works seamlessly with the STL algorithms

Compared to your common C program, STL has containers that have a more understandable interface than your in-house containers. This is an advantage for your future co-workers, who will catch up faster on your codebase.

Also, the STL containers are well documented and understood; any question that you might have has already been answered, or one is able to answer your question[4].

Type-safety of STL containers saves you from common C errors that involve type casting from `void*`.

The compiler catches errors that you would otherwise have to scan with the debugger.

STL's code is already fast, because it's light on checks and exceptions. It also provides better chances for the optimiser to kick-in than most C code. Read more on that in the section on speed.

Here is a typical way to fill a linear container with data:

dynamic array	doubly-linked list	double-ended queue
`vector<int> v;` `v.push_back(10);`	`list<int> v;` `v.push_back(10);`	`deque<int> v` `v.push_back(10);`
`int last = v.back();` `v.pop_back();`	`int last = v.back();` `v.pop_back();`	`int last = v.back();` `v.pop_back();`
`assert (v.size()==0);` `assert (v.empty());`	`assert (v.size()==0);` `assert (v.empty());`	`assert (v.size()==0);` `assert (v.empty());`

Here's a way to fill an associative container:

---

[4] a good place to look for such questions is http://www.stackoverflow.com

binary tree	hash table
| ```
map<string, int> m;
m["May"] = 5;
m["January"] = 1;
a_assert (m.size() == 2);
int num = m["January"];
``` | ```
unordered_map<int> m;
m["May"] = 5;
m["January"] = 1;
a_assert (m.size() == 2);
int num = m["January"];
``` |

As you can see, the interface is homogeneous for common functions. This allows you to switch between containers with minimal changes to the user code. Type safety prevents you from overusing typecasts.

```
vector<int> v;
v.insert(10);          // OK
v.insert(3.1415);      // implicit conversion: 3 added
v.insert("Hello!");    // compiler error !
```

In iterating a container you can replace your for loops from:

dynamic array	linked-list
| ```
int_array *p = new_int_array();
int i;
for (i=0; i<p->len; i++) {
  foo (p[i]);
}
int_array_free(p);
``` | ```
linked_list *p = new_linked_list();
while (p) {
  foo (p->data);
  p = p->next;
};
linked_list_free(p);
``` |

into:

vector	list
| ```
vector<int> p;
vector<int>::iterator it;
for (it=p.begin(); it != p.end(); ++it ) {
  foo (*p);
}
``` | ```
list<int> p;
list<int>::iterator it;
for (it=p.begin(); it != p.end(); ++it ) {
  foo (*p);
}
``` |

Of course, you can still use the more traditional:

```
vector<int> p;
for (size_t i=0; i < p.size(); ++i) {
    foo ( p[i] );
}
```

The use of iterators for abstracting the container helps you write code that does not change when the container changes, and reads the same in all cases. Low-level housekeeping is reduced; the `vector/list` is freed automatically when it goes out of scope.

2.3 Step 3: Do not write raw for-loops

Adopting STL containers has some advantages, but it does not lead to direct gains on readability. After all, this

```
for (vector<int>::iterator it=v.begin(); it!=v.end(); ++it) {
    ...
}
```

is not better to read. First attempts to getting it right is often a difficult task, too.

The fact is that all for loops have the drawback that you have to decipher them:

- when you exit from the loop it is difficult to reason what the variables' state will be; a conditional `break` or `continue` is enough to make the task of comprehension tough.
- at least one variable is added to the function's scope (an iterator, a control flag, etc)
- the loop disrupts the top-down reading flow of the function
- bugs may be hidden in such a loop
- optimisation opportunities are lost; the loop is forcefully inlined, thereby not leaving the optimiser much control.

Let's see a few examples of how raw for-loops deprave us from understanding the problems in the code.

2.3.1 Example 1: readability problems in C

Consider the following code:

C version

```c
Polygon *getCommonPolygonBetweenEdges(Edge *edge1, Edge *edge2)
{
    PtrArray *polygons1, *polygons2;
    Polygon *common_polygon = NULL, *run_polygon;
    void *run_ent;
    int num_common_polygons = 0;
    polygons1 = ptr_array_new(0);
    polygons2 = ptr_array_new(0);
    FOR_EVERY_POLYGON(edge1, run_polygon,
            {
                    ptr_array_append_val(polygons1, run_polygon);
            });
    FOR_EVERY_POLYGON(edge2, run_polygon,
            {
                    ptr_array_append_val(polygons2, run_polygon);
            });
    ptr_array_unique(polygons1);
    ptr_array_unique(polygons2);
    RUN_PTR_ARRAY(polygons1, run_ent,
            {
                    run_polygon = (Polygon *)run_ent;
                    if ( ptr_array_find_index(polygons2, run_polygon) >= 0 ) {
                            if ( !common_polygon && !num_common_polygons ) {
                                    common_polygon = run_polygon;
                                    num_common_polygons++;
                            } else if ( common_polygon != run_polygon ) {
                                    num_common_polygons++;
                            }
                    }
            });
    ptr_array_free_dum(polygons1);
    ptr_array_free_dum(polygons2);
    return (num_common_polygons > 0) ? common_polygon : NULL;
}
```

As you have guessed from its name, the function finds whether there is a common edge between two polygons in 3d-space.

The background information for this problem is:

- each `Polygon` is a list of `Edges`.
- each `Edge` contains a list of `Polygons` which share this edge.
- `PtrArray` is a library[5] that implements dynamic arrays.
- `FOR_EVERY_POLYGON` is a macro that encapsulates a loop that runs through the list of `Polygons` of an `Edge`.

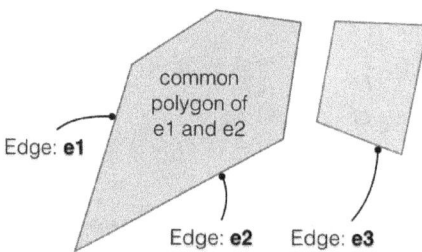

there is a common `Polygon` between `Edges` e1 and e2, but no common `Polygon` between `Edges` e2 and e3'

Now,

- can you honestly confirm that the function does what it says? if so,
- how long does it take you to understand it?
- would you say that it does its job efficiently?
- how eager would you be to undertake the task of adding some more functionality to it?

The code can be expressed by replacing the raw loops with the equivalent STL algorithms:

C++ version

```
Polygon *getCommonPolygonBetweenEdges(Edge *edge1, Edge *edge2)
{
    std::vector<Polygon*> polygons1, polygons2;
    std::vector<Polygon*> common_polygons;

    FOR_EVERY_POLYGON(edge1, run_polygon,
        {
                polygons1.push_back(run_polygon);
        });
    FOR_EVERY_POLYGON(edge2, run_polygon,
        {
                polygons2.push_back(run_polygon);
        });
    std::sort(polygons1);
```

---

[5]it is very similar to this one: http://enchantia.com/software/ace/assembler/ptrarray.c

```cpp
    std::sort(polygons2);
    std::set_intersection (polygons1.begin(), polygons1.end(),
                           polygons2.begin(), polygons2.end(),
                           std::back_inserter(common_polygons));

    return (num_common_polygons.empty()) ? NULL : common_polygon.front();
}
```

I have only tried to produce an equivalent code, without optimising, or changing the data structures of `Polygon` or `Edge`. Just the internals of the function. `vector` is the equivalent of the `PtrArray`, only more type-safe.

Notice how

- all the *noisy* local variables (`common_polygon`, `run_polygon`, `run_ent`, `num_common_polygons`) have vanished, due to the removal of the `for` loop.
- the complicated `if-else-if`, which was hard to reason about, is gone.
- the introduction of `vector` as an equivalent container has reduced the amount of housekeeping (allocation/deallocation), and the line count.

Due to the use of the standard algorithm (`set_intersection`) the code *reveals its intention better*, and it can therefore be *reviewed*.

In fact, *only now* can one point out that it is not necessary to sort both arrays and find their intersection in order to find a common edge between the polygons. It suffices to sort one and traverse the other to search the first.

The same result can be gotten by this code:

faster C++ version

```cpp
Polygon *getCommonPolygonBetweenEdges(Edge *edge1, Edge *edge2)
{
    std::vector<Polygon*> polygons1, polygons2;
    std::vector<Polygon*> common_polygons;

    FOR_EVERY_POLYGON(edge1, run_polygon,
        {
                polygons1.push_back(run_polygon);
        });
    FOR_EVERY_POLYGON(edge2, run_polygon,
        {
                polygons2.push_back(run_polygon);
        });
```

```
    std::sort(polygons2);

    std::vector<Polygon*>::iterator it;
    it = std::find_if( polygons1.begin(), polygons1.end(),
                       is_in_vector(polygons2) );


    return (it == polygons1.end()) ? NULL : *it;
}
```

So, you can see that it is raw loops that

- hide the intent of the code and
- you cannot reason about correctness or speed

Whereas with algorithms

- you can express intent directly
- you make the code readable, understandable, reviewable and therefore maintainable.

To take this one step further, I have changed the data structures to use a std::list of polygons, instead of the in-house implementation of the linked-list. This way, you can see the extra advantages you can get if you use STL containers, too.

even better C++ version

```
bool getCommonPolygonBetweenEdges(Edge *edge1, Edge *edge2)
{
    std::vector<Polygon*> edge2_polygons = edge2->polygons;

    std::sort(edge2_polygons);

    return std::any_of (edge1->polygons.begin(), edge1->polygons.end(),
                        is_in_vector(edge2_polygons));
}
```

While simplifying the code, I noticed that returning the pointer of some common polygon is not much of information. Indeed, looking at the calls of the function, no one ever used the return value – they all checked for existence of a common polygon.

It is worth mentioning that

- I haven't changed neither the abstract data structures, nor the logic of the solution. I merely detected redundant actions and allocations.
- I did not use object oriented techniques or any fancy way of thinking. I used the same logic flow, as a C function, but replaced loops with algorithms.

Finally, note that you cannot tell whether the `edge1->polygons` is a `list`, or a `vector`. In fact, the programmer is free to experiment with other data structures easily, without changing this function.

2.3.2 Example 2: readability problems in C++

C++ raw loops also suffer from readability. Consider the following function snippet:

original code with raw-loops

```cpp
{
    // Remove the pages that are in the range from active pages
    BlockMap::iterator active_it = active_pages.upper_bound(addr);

    if (active_it != active_pages.begin()) {
        active_it--;
    }

    while (active_it != active_pages.end()) {
        size_t act_start = active_it->first;
        size_t act_end = act_start + active_it->second;

        if (act_start >= al_end) {
            break;
        }

        if ((act_start >= al_start && act_start <= al_end) && (act_end >= al_star\
t && act_end <= al_end)) {
            active_pages.erase(active_it++);
        } else {
            ++active_it;
        }
    }
}
```

`BlockMap` is a `map<size_t,size_t>`. Take a few minutes to comment on the correctness of this code. It is very hard to tell! So, is this a badly written piece of code?

There are good qualities in this code:

- There is a short summary in comments, that describes its purpose.
- The variable names are quite well written.
- There is no mix of high level and low level concepts.

So, what's wrong with it? One would be tempted to argue that the function is difficult to comprehend because it describes a complex procedure.

When I was faced with this code, I didn't know where to start to comprehend it. I simply couldn't understand it. I decided that if I simplified a loop I could unravel the mystery. Then I recognised the pattern[6] that erases entries from a map during a loop:

typical pattern that deletes items from a map, while iterating

```
it=container.begin();
while (it!=container.end())
{
    if(condition) {
        container.erase(it++);
    } else {
        ++it;
    }
}
```

The details of this loop are significant - change the `it++` into `++it` and the correctness is broken. But if you allow this code to get intertwined with the `if`'s, the next programmer who tries to add some logic to it can break it. And no one will be able to fix it, as no one will have a clue of its original purpose.

The best way to *indicate intent* is to replace the loops with STL algorithms:

equivalent code without raw-loops

```
{
    BlockMap::iterator active_it = active_pages.upper_bound(addr);
    if (active_it != active_pages.begin()) {
        active_it--;
    }

    to = std::find_if (active_it, active_pages.end(),
                       key_is_greater_than (al_end));
    erase_if (active_it, to, active_pages,
              key_and_value_are_between (al_start, al_end));
}
```

---

[6]http://stackoverflow.com/questions/4600567/how-can-i-delete-elements-of-a-stdmap-with-an-iterator

erase_if() is not an STL algorithm – I created it. Admittedly, the function reads better because some logic has been moved into another function. But this is not cheating, since erase_if(), is a highly reusable algorithm.

Notice how the use of algorithms has disentangled the conditions under which the loop breaks. The while-loop would break when a condition was met. This is captured by the find_if() algorithm.

Notice, again, how clarification of the loops now allows the question: "what on earth do the first three lines do?". It is *this* bit of code that does not make sense, even though it is written quite clearly.

Finally, it is *only now* that

- the code is reviewable.
- meaningful questions can be asked.
- opportunities to redesign can come up.
- discussions on correctness are possible.

 replace raw-loops with algorithms[7].

You should strive to use algorithms instead of writing raw for loops. It makes code so much more *readable*. This makes it possible to reason about *speed*, *correctness*, and *complexity*.

You can read how to do this in the sections on STL algorithms and Callable objects

Surprisingly enough, the code for erase_if() is:

implementation for erase_if() for std::map

```
template <typename Iter, typename Predicate, typename Key, typename Value>
void erase_if (Iter from, Iter to, map<Key,Value> &container, Predicate condition)
{
    while (from != to)
    {
        if (condition(*from)) {
            container.erase(from++);
        } else {
            ++from;
        }
    }
}
```

[7]this advice was first advocated by Sean Parent, in his inspiring speech, during *Going Native 2013*. You can watch it in: http://channel9.msdn.com/Events/GoingNative/2013/Cpp-Seasoning

2.4 Step 4: Algorithms should read like pseudocode

When an algorithm is described like pseudo-code, there is hardly ever any mention about the underlying data-structures. No statement is made on whether a `list`, a `dynamic array`, or a `binary tree` should be used.

With C++, it *is* possible to code in such a way.

Let's compare how you would write an algorithm in C, that accumulates numbers in an array:

```
int accumulate (int numbers[], int sz, int sum)
{
    int i;
    for (i=0; i<sz; i++) {
        sum += numbers[i];
    }
    return sum;
}
```

Now, what would you do if you had to accumulate the entries of a `binary tree`? or a `linked list`?

- would you *re-write* a version of `accumulate()` for the `tree` or the `list`? or
- would you *copy* the `tree` or `list` into an array and then call `accumulate()`?

well, people usually choose the path of least pain:

- if you're in a hurry, you copy the data into suitable data structure, and then move to the next task.
- if you have time, you rewrite the algorithm, find a clumsy name, like `accumulate_list()`, or `accumulate2()`, taking the risk of introducing bugs.
- If the algorithm is simple enough, you rewrite it in-place, where you need it.

> a really conscious programmer might even consider writing a macro for it–for reuse. Try writing a macro for as simple an algorithm as this one! Then, try to provide a nice API to call it!

Done that? Now what would you do if you needed to accumulate over a container of `doubles`?

But really, if you wanted to describe the algorithm to your colleague, you would write it like:

```
T accumulate (IT from, IT to, T sum)
{
    foreach entry in [from:to]
        sum += entry;
    return sum
}
```

well, the equivalent in C++ is:

```
template <typename T, typename IT>
inline
T accumulate (IT from, IT to, T sum)
{
    for (IT iter = from; iter != to; ++iter)
        sum += *iter;
    return sum;
}
```

Look how you can call it:

```
vector<int>    v;    int    sum = 5;    sum = accumulate (v.begin(), v.end(), sum);
list<double>   v;    double sum = 5;    sum = accumulate (v.begin(), v.end(), sum);
set<float>     v;    float  sum = 5;    sum = accumulate (v.begin(), v.end(), sum);
```

this allows you to replace the container types without changing user code.

2.4.1 How does that compare to a C function ?

readability
    apart from the first line that declares the `template` types, the rest is good-old C/C++ code – there is no special syntax, or characters like \, # or ## that you see in macros.

speed
    execution speed is definitely much faster than copying the container to an array. The function is marked as `inline`, allowing the optimiser to decide whether it should be inlined, or not. In C,

- if `accumulate()` was an `extern` function, the optimiser would not be able to optimise.

- if a *macro* was used, the function would have forcefully be inlined, but that might not be the best action to take, especially for functions longer than 2-3 lines.

size of executable
　　if `accumulate()` is implemented as an **extern** function:

- in C, the code remains in the executable, even if it is not called.

- in C++, the `template` function is instantiated only when it is used.

　　if `accumulate()` is implemented as **macro**:

- in C, the code is copied in every macro use.

- In C++, *some* calls of the `template` function may be inlined, while others will share a single instance of the function.

code reuse
　　only by using a macro (a well known bad practice) can you reuse an algorithm with different parameter types. Template provides a much better option.

2.5 Step 5: Make use of the roll/unroll behaviour

The pattern that is most predominant in programming is:

- Setup some state
- Do some work
- Clean up

Manual housekeeping of this repetitive task requires too much care and energy, from the programmer's side. Repetitive tasks sounds like a work that should be automated, rather than maintained manually.

2.5.1 Example: File Read/Write

This is the second most common example, after `Hello World!`.

writing a string to a file

```
FILE *fp = fopen("output.txt", "wt");
fprintf(fp, "Hello World");
fclose(fp);
```

The file handle, `fp`, is never used unless it has been initialised with `fopen()`. The resource must always be freed, and cannot be used after `fclose()`. It therefore has a limited *scope*.

It is very important to release the file handle – failure to do so, repeatedly, may cause your file system to block.

2.5.2 Example: OpenGL

In OpenGL you cannot put any vertices through the pipeline, unless you have declared what they'll be used for, using `glBegin()`. No shape is going to be drawn unless you conclude that the vertices are over, using `glEnd()`.

Here's an example of how to draw a single line:

drawing a line with vertices

```
glBegin(GL_LINES);              // initialize
glVertex3f(0.0, 0.0, 0.0);      // work
glVertex3f(15, 0, 0);
glEnd();                        // finalize
```

If, additionally, you wish to temporarily set the line thickness, it is wise that you declare it before start drawing, and set it back to the previous thickness, after you're done.

drawing a line with different thickness

```
GLfloat prev_line_width;
glGetFloatv(GL_LINE_WIDTH, &prev_line_width);
glLineWidth(15);                // change width

glBegin(GL_LINES);              // initialize
glVertex3f(0.0, 0.0, 0.0);      // work
glVertex3f(15, 0, 0);
glEnd();                        // finalize

glLineWidth(prev_line_width);   // resume width
```

Note that the order of actions should be reversed after the work has taken place.

2.5.3 Example: Filling a listview

Filling a listview can be a time-consuming task. You decide to temporarily set the mouse cursor to *busy* while filling takes place. You also want to turn off the *sorting* of the list, because sorting while you append in the list will delay the process.

adding items to a list-view

```
int prev_mouse_cursor, prev_sort_state;

prev_mouse_cursor = get_cursor();
set_cursor(BUSY);                        // change mouse cursor to 'busy'
prev_sort_state = get_sorting(list);
set_sorting(list, NO_SORT);              // turn off list sorting
...
item = add_item_to_list(list, text);     // work
...
set_sorting(list, prev_sort_state);      // resume sorting state
set_cursor(prev_mouse_cursor);           // resume mouse state
```

And notice how hairy things can get when the situation is *just slightly* more complicated: Let's assume that as you add items to the listview, you notice an invalid item, and you have to ask the user whether to continue adding items, or not.

breaking while adding items to a list-view

```
int prev_mouse_cursor, prev_sort_state;

prev_mouse_cursor = get_cursor();
set_cursor(BUSY);
prev_sort_state = get_sorting(list);
set_sorting(list, NO_SORT);
...
item = add_item_to_list(list, text);    // work
if (is_invalid(item))
{
    int prev_mouse_cursor_2 = get_cursor();
    set_cursor(ARROW);
    if (ask("bad item - should I continue?") == NO) {
        set_sorting(list, prev_sort_state);
        set_cursor(prev_mouse_cursor);
        return;
    }
```

```
        set_cursor(prev_mouse_cursor_2);
}
...
set_sorting(list, prev_sort_state);
set_cursor(prev_mouse_cursor);
```

2.5.4 Solution

In C++, the *initialize/finalize* concept is built into the language. The concept is called *constructor* and *destructor*. The constructor is called when an object is created, and the destructor is called when the object leaves out of scope. If many objects are created in the stack, **the destruction order is the reverse of the order that they were constructed.**

2.5.5 Example revisited: filling the listview

using *scoped-guards* to preserve state

```
ScopedCursor temporarily_set_cursor_to(BUSY);
ScopedSorting temporarily_set_sorting_state_to(list, NO_SORT);
...
item = add_item_to_list(list, text);    // work
if (is_invalid(item))
{
    ScopedCursor temporarily_set_cursor_to(ARROW);
    if (ask("bad item - should I continue?") == NO) {
        return;
    }
}
```

How simpler is that to read and maintain ?

- The temporarily_set_cursor_to and temporarily_set_sorting_state_to are merely *variables*, that will die after their scope ends, thereby rolling back their actions.
    - The memory footprint is exactly the same as the one with the C implementation.
    - Running time is exactly the same
    - The execution order is exactly the same.
- I've carefully named the variables so that they read like English.
- the struct's name, Scoped, is chosen so that it reminds of its lifetime.

What is the code that supports this automation ? It is simply a struct, that runs a function on construction, and another function when it goes out of scope[8] :

---

[8]this pattern is also termed as *RAII* (Resource Acquisition Is Initialisation). RAII is claimed to be a better solution than the *garbage collection*.

typical implementation of a scoped-guard

```
struct ScopedCursor
{
    int prev_cursor;

    ScopedCursor(int new_cursor) {      // on construction
        prev_cursor = get_cursor();
        set_cursor(new_cursor);
    }

    ~ScopedCursor() {                    // on destruction
        set_cursor(prev_cursor);
    }
};
```

Note: a more sophisticated implementation would take special care so that `ScopedCursor` is non-copyable[9]. That would make the compiler prevent the user from copying the scoped-guard. But this is beyond the scope of this book.

2.6 Step 6: Revamp your callback methods

Callbacks are predetermined actions that are taken when a particular event has occurred. Typically, callbacks are implemented using *function pointers*.

An classic example of a callback is the function that a button should call when it is pressed.

header for Button

```
// callback prototype
typedef void (*BtnPressedFuncPtr) (int button_id,
                                   const char *button_text,
                                   void *user_data);

struct Button {
    BtnPressedFuncPtr pressed_cbk;   // store fn pointer in structure
    void *user_data;                  // store external data for the callback
    ...
};

// API for setting callback
```

---
[9] http://stackoverflow.com/questions/2173746/how-do-i-make-this-c-object-non-copyable

```
void SetButtonPressedFunction (Button* btn,
                               BtnPressedFuncPtr function,
                               void *user_data);
```

A Button has to perform some action when it is pressed. The Button therefore stores the pointer of this function into its structure. When the Button is pressed, it calls this function. It passes data about the button's state, such as button_id and button_text. It also passes data set by the user, the user_data, so that the callback contains all the necessary information to perform this action.

Using this setup, we can set the callback to the Button like so:

printing a message whenever the button is pressed

```
void on_button_pressed (int button_id,
                        const char *button_text,
                        void *user_data)
{
    printf ("button %s was pressed!\n", button_text);
}

Window *w = create_window("window title");
Button *btn = create_button_in_window(w, "press here");
SetButtonPressedFunction(btn, on_button_pressed, NULL); // no special data
```

user_data are necessary whenever the callback function needs to perform something more useful than just a printf(). In such a case, the user code would have to provide the data in the following fashion:

changing the window title when the button is pressed

```
struct ButtonPressedFunctionData {
    Window *target_window;
    const char *new_title;
};

ButtonPressedFunctionData* newButtonPressedData (Window *w, const char *title)
{
    ButtonPressedFunctionData *user_data = new ButtonPressedFunctionData;
    user_data->target_window = w;
    user_data->new_title = strdup(title);
    return user_data;
}
```

```
void deleteButtonPressedData (ButtonPressedFunctionData *user_data)
{
    if (user_data) free(user_data->new_title);
    delete user_data;
}

void on_button_pressed_change_title (int button_id,
                                     const char *button_text,
                                     void *user_data)
{
    ButtonPressedFunctionData *data = (ButtonPressedFunctionData*) user_data;

    SetWindowTitle (data->target_window, data->new_title);
}


// window set-up
Window *w = create_window("window title");
Button *btn = create_button_in_window(w, "press here");

ButtonPressedFunctionData *user_data =
        newButtonPressedData(w, "title changed");
SetButtonPressedFunction(btn,
                         on_button_pressed_change_title,
                         user_data); // provide data for callback

// when should user_data be deleted?
```

This case contains all the actions and considerations that a user faces when setting up a meaningful callback:

- a struct has to be defined for every callback that needs to be set. This is the user_data of the callback.
- user_data has to be allocated and passed as a void pointer, because Button has to store it somehow.
- user_data has to be released when the window no longed needs it. Who is responsible for deleting user_data ?
- in the callback, user_data is *cast* from a generic void pointer to some concrete pointer. This step is a constant generator of bugs.
- the callback *must* follow the function pointer's signature, even though we don't always care about the button_id or the button_text.

Creating this struct is quite painful:
> A *name* for the struct has to be invented. It is a useless name, but it still has to be a *good* name, otherwise it will cause confusion. The struct name simply fills up the namespace with noise.

Deleting the user_data requires some effort, too:
> Yet another callback needs to be setup, which will clear all the necessary window data, when the window is about to be deleted. This can involve creating yet another structure, which will contain all the pointers of all the user_data that need to be deleted when the window dies:

setting-up the deletion of user_data when the window closes

```
struct WindowClosedUserData {
    ButtonPressedFunctionData *btn_press_user_data;
    OtherWidgetUserData       *other_widget_user_data;
};

void on_window_closed_delete_all_user_data (Window *w, void *user_data)
{
    WindowClosedUserData *data = (WindowClosedUserData *) user_data;

    deleteButtonPressedData (data->btn_press_user_data);
    deleteOtherWidgetData (data->other_widget_user_data);

    delete data;
}


// window set-up
Window *w = create_window("window title");
Button *btn = create_button_in_window(w, "press here");

ButtonPressedFunctionData *user_data =
        newButtonPressedData(w, "title changed");
SetButtonPressedFunction(btn, on_button_pressed_change_title, user_data);

WindowClosedUserData *all_user_data = new WindowClosedUserData;
all_user_data->btn_press_user_data = user_data;
all_user_data->other_widget_user_data = ...;

SetWindowClosedFunction(w,
                        on_window_closed_delete_all_user_data,
                        all_user_data);
```

You may argue that *we don't need a separate* struct *for the* Button *callback data, and a separate one for each* Widget*'s callback data.*

Indeed, we could have only one large user_data for the whole Window, and this will reduce the number of support functions and data structures we write.

But that would increase the *rewrite* and *test* when the next similar window needs to be developed. The whole monolithic user_data structure would have to be developed from scratch, without any reusable components.

This is all unnecessary micromanagement again.

- The Button should clear up its own data when it goes out of scope. We shouldn't have to write explicit code for it.
- We shouldn't have to write explicit data structures for every callback we want.
- We shouldn't have to mimic the callback function prototype if we don't need all its parameters.

In STL, there is a construct which does all that: **std::function** can *store any callable object*, **and call it when needed.**

Here is how the same program looks like when you use the std::function:

header: Button stores a std::function instead of function pointer and user_data

```
#include <functional>

// callback prototype
typedef std::function <void (int button_id, const char *button_text)>
        BtnPressedFunc;

struct Button {
    BtnPressedFunc pressed_callback;      // no need to store the user_data
    ...
};

// API for setting callback
void SetButtonPressedFunction (Button* btn,
                               BtnPressedFunc function);
```

The function prototypes are still the same, only *leaner*, because we do not need to store the void pointer.

callback usage when std::function is involved

```
void on_button_pressed_change_title (Window *target_window, string new_title)
{
    SetWindowTitle(target_window, new_title.c_str());
}


Window *w = create_window("window title");
Button *btn = create_button_in_window(w, "press here");

SetButtonPressedFunction(
        btn,
        std::bind(on_button_pressed_change_title, w, "title changed"));

// no need for deleting data
SetWindowClosedFunction(w, ..., NULL);
```

It is std::function which provides all the ease of usage:

- std::function stores the arguments the callbacks need and deletes them when Button goes out of scope.
- std::bind acts as an adapter, converting the interface of on_button_pressed_change_title() into the signature that BtnPressedFunc demands.

  How do I read std::function ?

> std::function <void (int button_id, const char *button_text)>

denotes a function which takes an int and a const char* as input and returns void.

3 Efficiency advantages using STL and C++

When comparing the speed of a C program to the speed of the exactly the same program in C++, the chances are that C will perform better.

In practice, though, C++ allows you to write both faster and more readable code at the same time. The keys to understanding what really affects speed are *cache* and *branch prediction*.

Data or code that exists in cache can run at 100x faster[1]
> The processor can only access data that exist in the cache. If the data is not there, they are fetched from memory. This process is way too slow, and it freezes computations until the data is fetched.

Loops without branches, or where branch prediction is achieved can run 10x faster[2]
> Today's processors use techniques to pre-fetch data that may be used in pieces of code that is going to be executed later. If the processor's prediction is successful, then you will have the data in the CPU's registers when you reach the lines that need it. If you branch off and execute a different path than the expected one (e.g. through a conditional `break`, `continue`, `goto`) then the data are thrown away.

3.1 Templates are faster than macros

Take a code with a macro and a template function which contain the same code and run some timing tests, using a small testing program. The macro runs faster or at the same speed as the templated function. So why am I claiming the opposite?

Well, let's consider how one can implement a routine:

- using a function
- using a macro
- using a templated function

Quick sort is a good example to study.

---

[1] Watch Stroustrup's opening speech in Going Native 2012, skip to 44min40sec, http://channel9.msdn.com/Events/GoingNative/GoingNative-2012/Keynote-Bjarne-Stroustrup-Cpp11-Style

[2] http://stackoverflow.com/questions/11227809/why-is-processing-a-sorted-array-faster-than-an-unsorted-array

3.1.1 quick sort as a function

In C, you can sort a sequence using qsort() of <stdlib.h>

```
int compare_ids ( void *a, void *b ) {
    struct Element *p = (Element*) a;
    struct Element *q = (Element*) b;
    if (p->id == q->id) return 0;  // same
    if (p->id <  q->id) return 1;  // less
    return -1;                     // greater
}


Element array[];
...
qsort( array, array_size, sizeof(Element), compare_ids );
...
```

The problem with this approach is that the optimiser can only partly optimise, because qsort() is an external function and because it is disjoint from compare_ids(). Another problem is the use of function pointers – this dereference adds some unnecessary burden to the function. The other nuisance is that the use of void* for comparison is not type-safe.

3.1.2 quick sort as a macro

A macro implementation of quick sort looks like it gives the optimiser better chances of success, since all the code is available to the optimiser:

```
#define COMPARE_ELEMENT_IDS (a, b, result) {           \
    if      (a->id == b->id) result = 0;               \
    else if (a->id <  b->id) result = 1;               \
    else                     result = -1;

Element array[]
...
QSORT ( Element, array, array_size, COMPARE_ELEMENT_IDS );
...
```

This implementation forces all the code of quick sort to be inlined. No function calls or function pointers are involved here, so it appears that the code should run faster.

However, this solution entails a danger that can rarely be seen in a small unit test. In a real case, you may sort arrays in succession, like so:

```
for (...) {
   QSORT ( Element, array1, array1_size, COMPARE_ELEMENT_IDS );
   QSORT ( Element, array2, array2_size, COMPARE_ELEMENT_IDS );
   ids = find_common_entities (array1, array1_size, array2, array2_size);

   QSORT ( Element, array1, array1_size, COMPARE_ELEMENT_NAMES );
   QSORT ( Element, array2, array2_size, COMPARE_ELEMENT_NAMES );
   names = find_common_entities (array1, array1_size, array2, array2_size);
} }
```

This program has a bottleneck: there are too many copies of QSORT code inlined. This has the side effect that

- There is not enough space for all code of the loop inside the instruction cache. Each copy of QSORT can push instructions out of the cache.
- In processors where *instruction cache* and *data cache* are not separated, heavy inlining can also push data out of the cache.

Heavy inlining promotes cache misses, which is exactly the opposite of what people intend when they use macros.

In this case, we unintentionally choked the cache by inlining too much code. We could have achieve better performance if we used qsort(). Then, only one copy of qsort() would exist in the cache, leaving more space for other instructions.

Which implementation is faster though requires a separate study, on a case-by-case basis.

3.1.3 quick sort as a template

When you use a templated function, all the code exists in one translation unit[3], and therefore the optimiser can decide whether it should inline std::sort(), or compare_ids(), or both, or none of them.

---

[3]*translation unit* is essentially a .cpp file.

```
inline
bool compare_ids (const Element &a, const Element &b) {
    return a->id < b->id;
}

Element array[]
...
std::sort ( array, array+array_size, compare_ids );
...
```

3.1.4 conclusion

In C we have explicit control of whether we want to inline functions or not. This is not a good situation. No programmer should constantly have to choose between a macro or a function. The best should always be chosen for them. Micromanagement on such a level is really a waste of time. Manual choice, even under the assumption that the programmer *really* knows, is fiction, because *the best* in one platform might not be good in another. To make things even worse, programmers don't usually have the choice of whether to use a macro or a function; they choose whichever is available, or whichever fits their style. This is a poor situation. Yet, so many people will advocate that C is faster...

In C++ we can pass control to the optimiser, to choose whether to inline or not. This is done by using a templated function. There is no matter of style here – a templated function is used just like a normal function. If the programmer has found that the optimiser is wrong, he can then choose to use a macro or a function, explicitly, choosing to inline, or not to. But usually he doesn't have to.

Therefore, C++ templates offer the programmer a more readable interface, and at the same time produce code that optimises better.

3.2 Efficiency of std::string vs char*

3.2.1 low-level strings

A string in a char* is a very compact structure. You always access the string via a pointer. Low level strings contain no redundant information. If you need to know its size, you pay strlen() $\mathcal{O}(n)$ to find it. To do an insertion you have to know whether there's enough memory allocated.

3.2.2 std::string and QString

std::string is self-sufficient. It manages its own memory allocations. It knows its size, which gives some speed advantage. The great speed advantage comes when using small strings. Small strings (less than 16 characters long) are stored inside the structure[4], not referenced via a pointer. This means that there are no extra costs in copying such strings. Also, such strings are in the stack, and items in the stack are practically always in the CPU cache. This makes `std::string` faster than low-level strings, in such cases.

Up until `tr1` of C++, strings could employ the *copy-on-write*[5] pattern. This means that the string buffer is not copied, unless a change is made to the string. This allows you to make copies of the `string`, but without copying the string buffer. Although speed can also be achieved by passing pointers to low-level strings, it is not safe to do so, because the string passed to a function might be changed by another function that shares the same pointer.

3.2.3 strings with rope data structure

Not all implementations of STL make use of copy-on-write pattern. `QString`[6] does though, and it is a perfectly reasonable alternative to use, with more useful member functions. Surprisingly, since C++11, the *copy-on-write* is disallowed by the standard[7], because it is not efficient for multi-threading[8]. Fortunately, the new implementations are free to use the rope structure[9], which has proved its value in other languages. The *rope* data structure is really efficient in *insertion, deletion and concatenation* (which have a complexity of $\mathcal{O}(log(n))$, compared to $\mathcal{O}(n)$ of typical string implementations). Moreover, the rope structure allows for large string to be broken up in smaller chunks, thus not requiring the memory manager to find huge lumps of consecutive memory to allocate a very large string.

3.2.4 conclusion

`std::string` is yet another example of how **employing STL and C++ can make your code faster with future compiler versions**. Both the C++ standard and the STL implementations evolve, adopting newer techniques which brings better performance without changing your code[10]. On the contrary, if you program using low-level structures, there is practically no way your program can ever gain any extra speed, ever.

3.3 Order of complexity does not reflect performance

Colleges still teach students to prefer binary search trees (BST) over arrays because of the $\mathcal{O}(log(n))$ *search complexity*, compared to $\mathcal{O}(n)$ of arrays. *Insertion complexity* is the same, plus the tree has

---

[4]this occurs in many STL implementations, but not in every. Read more about this, in *Effective STL, Item 15* by Scott Meyers.

[5]http://en.wikibooks.org/wiki/More_C%2B%2B_Idioms/Copy-on-write

[6]QString is a part of the widely used, free, cross-platform library, *Qt*.

[7]http://stackoverflow.com/questions/12199710/legality-of-cow-stdstring-implementation-in-c11

[8]*copy-on-write* is implemented in terms of a reference counted string buffer. This means that the counter must be protected by a mutex, leading to poor performance in multi-threaded use.

[9]http://en.wikipedia.org/wiki/Rope_(data_structure)

[10]after all, backwards compatibility is a *feature* for C++

its elements already sorted. This sounds so great that people are always tempted into using sets or maps.

Linked lists are also popular, because the $\mathcal{O}(1)$ insertion and deletion sounds appealing.

The problem with these data structures, apart from taking up more space, is that the actual data is scattered in memory. The side-effect of this, is that data access is dominated by cache misses.

vector, on the other hand, is a compact representation of data. If you access one entry, many more will exist in the same page. Access to these elements is effectively instant. In fact, operations over elements on a vector can be two to three orders of magnitude faster than the equivalent on a set or a list. This means that on a vector you can run a $\mathcal{O}(n^2)$ algorithm faster than an $\mathcal{O}(log(n))$ on a binary tree.

This means that vector should be the default container to use, before trying another one.

One extra hint that may prompt you to rethink of vector in case you already have an implementation with a different container, is to see whether you run a for-loop over a range of its elements. Sequential access of data of a set, or a list can be hundreds of times slower, although we all like to think of them as an $\mathcal{O}(1)$ operation.

Watch to Stroustrup's key-note speech in Going Native 2012[11], (jump to 44'40"), about efficiency of C++.

Read the chapter on cache issues, to get an understanding on when cache misses happen, and how you can program your way around it.

3.4 Old speed issues that don't exist anymore

In the early 90's, C++ received a lot of criticism because a lot of copying was taking place, mainly through implicit calls of copy-constructors. Ten years later, this flaw has been fixed.

3.4.1 returning containers

In order to prevent superfluous copying, the C-style way of returning large structures had been adopted:

---

[11] http://channel9.msdn.com/Events/GoingNative/GoingNative-2012/Keynote-Bjarne-Stroustrup-Cpp11-Style

old style of returning large data-structures

```
void get_fibonacci_terms (vector<int> *dest, int num_terms);

...
vector<int> fib_sequence;
get_fibonacci_terms (&fib_sequence, 500);   // get the first 500 terms
...
```

But, with the latest advancements in return-value-optimisation[12], it is now advised to use the more readable style:

modern style for returning large data-structures

```
vector<int> fibonacci_terms (int num_terms);

...
vector<int> fib_sequence = fibonacci_terms(500);   // get the first 500 terms
...
```

The compiler can now create optimal code, where the return value is not copied to a temporary variable before it is returned. This can be achieved under particular (but not uncommon) circumstances: just declare the variable whose value is to be returned, *first*:

to achieve RVO, declare the return variable *first*

```
vector<int> fibonacci_terms (int num_terms) {
        vector<int> ret_value;
        ...
        // fill ret_value
        ...
        return ret_value;
}
```

Return value optimisation *will not* happen in if you return different objects on some path of execution:

---

[12]http://en.wikipedia.org/wiki/Return_value_optimization

RVO fails in this case

```
vector<int> fibonacci_terms (int num_terms) {
        vector<int> ret_value;
        vector<int> no_values;

        if (num_terms <= 0) {
                return no_values;
        } else {
                ...
                // fill ret_value
                ...
                return ret_value;
        }
}
```

 In C++11, efficient returning of large data-structures can be explicitly instructed by the programmer, even in cases where the optimiser would not achieve RVO. This is done by move semantics[13].

3.4.2 copying between vectors

Copying an array of primitive data types[14] to another array is fast if you employ memmove() and memcpy().

Older versions of std::copy would follow the slow path to copying:

```
std::copy (from, to, dest);
```

would run a for-loop through the range [from,to), copying each element to dest, one-by-one. This was suboptimal, and was for quite some time a cause for sarcasm against C++.

Latest STL implementations have template specialisations for ints, floats, pointers, that uses these system functions when copying. In fact, the std::copy() implementations are so sophisticated that they know when to use memcpy() and when to use the slower, but safer memmove(). There is no way you can trust that the programmer will choose right, between memmove() and memcpy()[15].

 Employing STL algorithms gives you hope that the same code may run faster with future STL libraries. Using self-crafted code guarantees that this code will never run any faster in the future.

---

[13]http://www.cprogramming.com/c++11/rvalue-references-and-move-semantics-in-c++11.html
[14]like int, float, double, or pointer
[15]http://stackoverflow.com/questions/4415910/memcpy-vs-memmove

3.5 map vs unordered_map

map is implemented as a red-black binary-search-tree in STL. Since tr1, hash tables are available in STL, under the name of unordered_map.

The unordered_map is the associative container that you should need in most cases, rather than a map. Most times, people use map in order to make sure that an element has already been inserted to the container. They hardly ever need the elements in ascending order.

Searching for a key, **in the worst case**, requires

- *amortised* $\mathcal{O}(1)$ time for an unordered_map.
- $\mathcal{O}(log(n))$ time for a map or set.

In fact, as measurements[16] show, searching for a key takes **on average**

- 1.3 comparisons for an unordered_map.
- $log(n-1)$ comparisons[17] for a map.

One extra feature, is that unordered_map has smaller memory overhead that binary-search-trees.

You should always consider using unordered_map or unordered_set, before a map or set. Only use map or set if sorting is necessary.

---

[16] http://cpp-tip-of-the-day.blogspot.gr/2013/11/how-does-stdunorderedset-compare-to.html

[17] this is in the optimal case, where the binary tree is *perfectly* balanced. In such a tree, *half* of the tree nodes are leaves, taking $log(n)$ comparisons to find them.

4 Am I doing it right ?

Sometimes, you think you follow the steps described in this book, but you do not feel comfortable with the resulting code. So I shall provide some examples of why things turn out bad, and provide different ways of looking at it.

4.1 bind-mania

Overuse of `bind()` is a typical tendency when learning this new feature. Let's study this example, where there is a typical pattern in Qt library, which converts `QString` to `const char*`:

typical pattern to getting a char* from a QString

```
void store_to_list ( QListView *list, const char *label, int column )
{
        QListViewItem *lvi = list->appendItem();
        lvi->setText (label, column);
}


void fill_list (QListView *list)
{
        vector<QString> names;   // = { "Jason", "Nick", "James" }

        for (int i=0; i<names.size(); i++) {
              store_to_list (list,
                             names[i].toUtf8().constData(),
                             2);
        }
}
```

People tend to like `bind()`, because they see all the code that the algorithm calls. Here's how one tried to replace the raw-loop with an algorithm:

overusing `std::bind()`

```
void fill_list (QListView *list)
{
        vector<QString> names;   // = { "Jason", "Nick", "James" }

        for_each (names.begin(), names.end(),
                bind (store_to_list,
                      list,
                      bind (&QByteArray::constData,
                            bind (&QString::toUtf8, placeholders::_1)),
                      2));
}
```

Clearly this is not just an overkill, it is an anti-pattern.

 Remember

You should only use the tools described in this book to make code more readable.

4.1.1 rationalising usage of `bind`

A more sensible solution would be to move the boring pattern of converting a `QString` to `const char*`, inside a function. This is a sensible choice because the function could be used over and over in many occasions.

more rational use of `std::bind()`

```
const char *to_const_char (QString s) {
        return s.toUtf8().constData();
}

void fill_list (QListView *list)
{
        vector<QString> names;   // = { "Jason", "Nick", "James" }

        for_each (names.begin(), names.end(),
                bind (store_to_list,
                      list,
                      bind (to_const_char, placeholders::_1),
```

```
                                    2));
        }
}
```

Another solution would be to make another function, like `store_to_list()`, which accepts a QString:

reducing the use of `std::bind()`

```
const char *to_const_char (QString s) {
        return s.toUtf8().constData();
}

void store_qstring_to_list (QListView *list, QString str, int column) {
        store_to_list (list, to_const_char(str), column);
}

void fill_list (QListView *list)
{
        vector<QString> names;   // = { "Jason", "Nick", "James" }

        for_each (names.begin(), names.end(),
                bind (store_qstring_to_list,
                    list,
                    placeholders::_1,
                    2));
        }
}
```

The sensible thing to do would be to use the same name, `store_to_list()`, in both functions, since they do the same thing. Unfortunately, `bind()` does not work well with function overloading, so I had to use a different name, `store_qstring_to_list()` instead of overloading `store_to_list()`.

4.1.2 replacing `bind` with function object

You could try to use a function object for more readability:

function object provides readability

```cpp
struct store_string_to_list {
        store_string_to_list (QListView *list, int column)
                : m_list(list), m_column(column)
        {
        }

        void operator() (QString str) {
                store_to_list ( m_list, to_const_char(str), m_column );
        }

        QListView *m_list;
        int m_column;
};

void fill_list (QListView *list)
{
        vector<QString> names;   // = { "Jason", "Nick", "James" }

        for_each (names.begin(), names.end(),
                store_string_to_list (list, 2));
        }
}
```

The function objects provide readability. They also promote reusability. In this case, you could use the same function object in other loops, without rewriting the complicated `bind` construct.

But what if in the other loops, you had containers of `std::string` or `QString` or `char*` ?

You can make the function object flexible to other types of input by overloading `operator()`. If you do so, the same function object can be called by any loop, whether it uses `QString`, `std::string`, or `const char*`. Using it with many types of input may eventually pay for the extra effort you put into building this function object.

function object with overloaded operator()s for flexibility

```
struct store_string_to_list {
        store_string_to_list (QListView *list, int column)
                : m_list(list), m_column(column)
        {
        }

        void operator() (QString str) {
                store_to_list ( m_list, to_const_char(str), m_column );
        }

        void operator() (std::string str) {
                store_to_list ( m_list, str.c_str(), m_column );
        }

        void operator() (const char *str) {
                store_to_list ( m_list, str, m_column );
        }

        QListView *m_list;
        int m_column;
};
```

4.1.3 implicit conversion

As you may suspect, although store_string_to_list() is a functor that might be used in a couple of places, it is not common enough to compensate for the effort we put into refining it. At the end of the day, store_string_to_list() is not the recurring pattern, *conversion* from QString to const char* *is*.

So, I'll extract out this pattern, and turn it into struct which can convert any kind of string type into a const char*. Let's call it CharPtr.

conversion is the recurring pattern

```cpp
struct CharPtr {
        string m_str;       // store string in a neutral format

        // implicit conversion from QString
        CharPtr(QString str)                : m_str(to_const_char(str)) { }

        // implicit conversion from char *
        CharPtr(const char *str)            : m_str(str) { }

        // construct from another string
        CharPtr(const std::string& str)     : m_str(str) { }

        // typecast operator - converts into 'const char *'
        operator const char *() {
                return m_str.c_str();
        }
};

struct store_string_to_list {
        store_string_to_list (QListView *list, int column)
                : m_list(list), m_column(column)
        {
        }

        void operator() (CharPtr str) {     // accept any string type
                store_to_list ( m_list, str, m_column );
        }

        QListView *m_list;
        int m_column;
};

void fill_list (QListView *list)
{
        vector<QString> names;  // = { "Jason", "Nick", "James" }

        for_each (names.begin(), names.end(),
                store_string_to_list (list, 2));    // same way to invoke
        }
}
```

Implicit conversion classes[1] is a pretty sophisticated idiom of C++. CharPtr is used only for building a temporary string out of any type of strings, and then to cast it to const char* on every request. Ability to build from any type of string is provided by its constructors. Casting to a given type is provided by its *typecast operator*.

converter accepts any type of string and implicitly casts it to const char* when needed

```
CharPtr a = "converts";            // generate from char *
CharPtr b = std::string("all");    // generate from std::string
CharPtr c = QString("strings");    // generate from QString

cout << a << " " << b << " " << c; // implicit cast to 'const char *'
```

 Use idioms wisely:

Although I have described many ways of expressing the same thing, you should be wise and choose the one which best promotes *readability* and *reusability* in your case.

- Do not put strange idioms into the face of the reader. Remember, everything is done to enhance reading experience.
- Do not sacrifice speed, where speed is critical.

4.1.4 lambda functions

Last, but not least, C++11 code can use the more direct *lambda function*:

expressing yourself directly, using *lambda function*

```
void fill_list (QListView *list)
{
        vector<QString> names;  // = { "Jason", "Nick", "James" }

        for_each (names.begin(), names.end(),
                [=] (QString str) {
                        store_to_list (list, to_const_char(str), 2);
                }
        )
}
```

---

[1]http://www.cplusplus.com/doc/tutorial/typecasting/

function object or lambda function ?

lambda function is likely to make `bind()` obsolete in the coming years. But the *function object* still has some advantages.

- **the function object**
    requires some typing, but it is highly reusable, and reads nicely,
- **the lambda function**
    needs less typing, but it is a one-off function (not reusable). You have direct supervision of its internals.

4.2 loving low-level data structures

Although C++ is a multi-paradigm language, it does not mean that we have to mimic other languages' idioms. When I was studying the following snippet, I felt there were code smells.

example of a non-native C++ style

```
#include "WidgetInfoData.h"
#include "gui_lib.h"
#include "WidgetsImplementation.h"

class PushButtonData: public WidgetInfoData
{
    public:
            PushButtonData(int id, int show, int order, const char *label);
            ~PushButtonData();

            WidgetType getWidgetType(void) { return PUSH_BUTTON; }
            void setText(const char *text);
            void setPixmapFile(const char *pixmap_file);

            void *createWidget(void *layout);
            void createListImgOfWidget(void *item, int column);
            int getNumOfImages(void) { return 1; }
    private:
            char *_text;
            char *_pixmap_file;
};
```

This code has all the ingredients demonstrated by most texts on object oriented programming.

- there is inheritance
- there is encapsulation of data in a *private* section
- there are *setters* and no *getters*, which implies a usage plan; I expect to
  - *set()* some attributes, and then
  - call a *build()*, *make()*, or *create()*.

However, this code is plagued with verbosity.

4.2.1 in C++ you do not have to declare *no arguments* with `void`

This is not so important, but it is useless noise. Remove it.

`void` parameter is a C-style declaration

```
WidgetType getWidgetType(void) { return PUSH_BUTTON; }
WidgetType getWidgetType() { return PUSH_BUTTON; }
```

4.2.2 in C++ you do not have to inline functions in the class definition

Defining functions inside the class definition is a Java habit, induced by the plethora of books which teach OOP using Java or C#.

Inlining functions would make sense if you had to provide maximum speed to the function. Otherwise, it is just noisy code, and potentially risky[2].

In our case, the class is designed to produce widgets with icons. Inlining will give no speed benefits, because we will not possibly create millions of widgets to cause an observable delay. Therefore, I moved the implementation to the `.cpp` file.

remove unnecessary inline functions

```
WidgetType getWidgetType() { return PUSH_BUTTON; }
WidgetType getWidgetType();
int getNumOfImages(void) { return 1; }
int getNumOfImages();
```

Then, magically, there is no more need to `#include` all headers

---

[2] read this article: http://cpp-tip-of-the-day.blogspot.gr/2014/04/inline-static-extern-functions-and.html

removing inline functions from the header, reduces dependencies

```
#include "WidgetInfoData.h"
#include "gui_lib.h"
#include "WidgetsImplementation.h"
```

4.2.3 low-level data require construction and destruction

The *destructor* looks like it exists only for dealing with the `char*`. Indeed, a quick look at the implementation file reveals a lot of boilerplate code.

boilerplate code written because of low-level data

```
PushButtonData::PushButtonData(int id, int show, int order, const char *label)
    : WidgetInfoData(id, show, order, label)
{
    _text = NULL;
    _pixmap_file = NULL;
}

PushButtonData::~PushButtonData(void)
{
    if (_text) free(_text);
    if (_pixmap_file) free(_pixmap_file);
}

void PushButtonData::setText(const char *text)
{
    if (_text) free(_text);
    _text = text ? strdup(text) : NULL;
}
```

There is absolutely no use for keeping low-level constructs. We did not need to store a *pointer to a char*. What we needed to store was a *string*.

Therefore, using a `string` instead of `char*`,

- the *constructor* is simplified.
- the *destructor* is no longer needed – the `string` frees itself when it goes out of scope.
- `setText()` and `setPixmapFile()` have no real purpose in this context. The strings could become *public* without affecting robustness of this code.

removing functions with high administration costs

```
#include <string>
#include "WidgetInfoData.h"

class PushButtonData: public WidgetInfoData
{
    public:
        PushButtonData(int id, int show, int order, const char *label);

        WidgetType getWidgetType();

        void *createWidget(void *layout);
        void createListImgOfWidget(void *item, int column);
        int getNumOfImages();

        std::string _text;
        std::string _pixmap_file;
};
```

The header is now free from noise. The reviewers can now do their job, assessing the class' purpose in the overall design. Meaningful discussions are now easier to achieve.

4.3 for_each everywhere

During the initial stages of converting raw-loops to algorithms, programmers often fall into the trap of seeing everything as a `for_each()` loop.

the raw-loop that is to be replaced

```
vector<int> vec; // = { 1, 2, 3, 4, 5, 6, 7, 8 }
set<int> t;
for (size_t i=0 ; i<vec.size(); i++)
{
    if (x % 2) continue;
    t->insert(vec[i]);
}
```

 continue and break are as good as goto statements.
This makes it important to vanish this raw-loop.

Many times, replacements end up like this:

naive replacement of a raw-loop with an algorithm

```
struct add_even_number {
        set<int> *m_dest;

        add_even_number (set<int> *dest)
              : m_dest(dest) {}

        void operator() (int x) {
                if ((x % 2)==0) m_dest->insert(x);
        }
};

vector<int> vec; // = { 1, 2, 3, 4, 5, 6, 7, 8 }
set<int> t;
for_each (vec.begin(), vec.end(), add_even_number(&t));
```

Although the caller code reads fairly well, it requires a disproportional function object. One extra thing to notice is that this function object does more than one job. It checks a condition, and it inserts to a set. Also, it is very coupled to set<int> and vector<int>. Because of this, the chances of this function object of getting reused are pretty low.

- The most important key to replacing raw-loops is to *learn the STL algorithms.*
- The next most important key to writing reusable code is to detect which is the *reusable function.*

What the programmer want to achieve is copy all but the odd values. In other words:
    copy if even, or

    copy if not odd.

This can be achieved by

using the correct algorithm improves decoupling, reading and reusability

```
bool is_even (int x) {
        return ((x % 2)==0);
}

vector<int> vec; // = { 1, 2, 3, 4, 5, 6, 7, 8 }
set<int> t;
copy_if (vec.begin(), vec.end(), inserter(t, t.begin()), is_even);
```

In this formulation the *condition* (`is_even`) is decoupled from the *insertion*, which is handled by a different object (the `inserter`), Apart from making both objects clearer, it makes both the *condition* and *inserter* much more reusable.

 Making your functions or objects do *one and only one* job greatly increases its chances for being reused. Using STL algorithm helps in decoupling functions, thus improving reusability.

4.4 replicating STL algorithms

After discovering how helpful algorithms are, people want to employ them for the data structures of their classes. But they do not want to make their data structures *public*. So they replicate or imitate STL algorithms.

imitating STL algorithm to keep variables private

```
class Polygon {
        private:
                vector<Point> points;
        public:
                template<class Func>
                Func for_each_point (Func);

                template<class Func>
                Func for_each_edge (Func);

                // other public members here
};
```

This solution works fine in that it does not expose the internal structure of the class, and allows the programmer to change the class without affecting user code. However, it suffers from lack of expressiveness, as explained in the issue above.

Sooner or later, you will need to implement a `find_if_point()`, a `transform_point()`, `copy_point()` and so on. But these algorithms have already been written for you. So, why replicate STL algorithms ?

 The secret for providing access to the data of an object, without exposing its internal data structure is to export *iterator* to the data.

Here's how you would give access to the `Points` held by `Polygon` without exposing the data structures:

exporting iterators to the class' data is the best approach

```
class Polygon {
        private:
                vector<Point> points;
        public:
                typedef vector<Point>::iterator PointIterator;

                PointIterator begin_point();
                PointIterator end_point();

                friend class EdgeIterator;

                EdgeIterator begin_edge();
                EdgeIterator end_edge();

                // other public members here
};
```

By exporting iterators, the user can access the vertices like:

```
Polygon::PointIterator it =
        std::max_element( polygon.begin_point, polygon.end_point(), compare_x_dir);
```

This allows for better expressiveness than `for_each_point()`.

`PointIterator` is just an iterator to the internal data structure. This is easy to implement with just a `typedef` because the data it represents (a container of points) maps directly to the structure held internally.

The `EdgeIterator`, on the other hand, is a more complex case. The internal structure of the `Polygon` does not store edges. `EdgeIterator` should behave like a *pointer-to-edges*. Therefore, is must be a class which provides an iterator interface, but convert data from the container.

The iterator should *at least* be able to

advance to the next edge:	`++it` and `it++`	pre- and post-increment operator
be dereferenced:	`*it`	dereference operator
compare with another iterator:	`while (it != end) {...}`	equivalence operator
be assigned:	`it = begin`	assignment operator

The *edge* which the iterator returns should give access to change the Points of the polygon. Therefore, an `Edge` should contain references to two Points:

`EdgeIterator` returns `Edge`, which is just a structure of two `Point`s

```cpp
struct Edge {
    Point &first;
    Point &second;

    Edge (Point &a, Point &b)   // convenience constructor
        : first(a), second(b) {}
};
```

This is the way I chose to implement `EdgeIterator`. It contains the minimum interface[3] that a custom iterator has to support.

minimum interface for an iterator

```cpp
class EdgeIterator : public std::iterator<std::input_iterator_tag, Edge> {
    private:
        vector<Point>::iterator m_iter;   // the state
        vector<Point> *m_orig;
    public:
        EdgeIterator(const vector<Point>* ref);
        EdgeIterator(const EdgeIterator* other);  // copy constructor

        EdgeIterator& operator++();         // pre-increment operator
        EdgeIterator  operator++(int);      // post-increment operator

        EdgeIterator& operator=(const EdgeIterator& rhs);  // assignment

        bool operator==(const EdgeIterator& rhs) const;    // equivalence
```

---
[3] find more custom-iterator examples in http://www.cplusplus.com/reference/iterator/iterator/

```
        bool operator!=(const EdgeIterator& rhs) const;

        Edge operator* ();                    // dereference operators
        const Edge operator* () const;
};
```

As you can see, EdgeIterator also contains a *reference* to the originating container, the vector itself. This is dictated by the fact that the Polygon is a closed shape, and therefore the last edge is composed by the *last* and *first* points of the Polygon. So I needed a way of to get access to the *first* iterator of points, when the *end* is reached.

The dereference operator returns a structure containing references to two successive Points:

implementation of the dereference operator

```
Edge EdgeIterator::operator* ()
{
        vector<Point>::iterator curr = m_iter;
        vector<Point>::iterator next = curr;
        ++next;
        if (next == m_orig->end())        // end is reached
                next = m_orig->begin();

        return Edge (*curr, *next);
}
```

The whole implementation can be found in my blog[4].

 creating custom iterators requires some effort, but it pays well for classes that are to be widely used.

---

[4]http://cpp-tip-of-the-day.blogspot.gr/2014/05/building-custom-iterators.html

Learning the details

5 Expressing intent using STL algorithms

STL algorithms abstract out the most common patterns of programming, like

- iteration
- copying
- searching
- sorting

Without using algorithms, one would resort to repeatedly writing boilerplate code like this:

typical code for finding the minimum element of a range

```
int numbers[] = { 2, 4, 5, 6, 7, 8, 9 };
int sz = sizeof(numbers)/sizeof(int);

int min_number = MAX_INT;
bool min_found = false;
for (int i=0; i<sz; ++i)
{
        if (numbers[i] < min_number) {
                min_number = numbers[i];
                min_found = true;
        }
}

if (min_found) {
        cout << "minimum number is " << min_number;
}
```

where

- there is a chance of getting it wrong, and even worse finding it out too late.
- the namespace is polluted by the iterators and control variables, like `i` and `min_found`.
- having the loop exposed allows future writers to stick in other bits of code, making the loop incomprehensible

Instead of doing this, you can use the `std::min_element()` algorithm:

using STL to find the minimum element of a range

```
int numbers[] = { 2, 4, 5, 6, 7, 8, 9 };
int sz = sizeof(numbers)/sizeof(int);

int *min_number = min_element(numbers, numbers+sz);

if (min_number != numbers+sz) {
        cout << "minimum number is " << *min_number;
}
```

The advantages of using an abstract STL algorithm are (apart from addressing the disadvantages of the raw loop):

- the intention is clearly expressed.
- the line count has decreased
- the algorithm is more efficient than almost any hand-written implementation

5.1 Customising algorithms with comparators

For standard datatypes, like `int`, `double`, and pointers, *comparison* is built in the language. But for most cases, a comparison function is needed to define the criterion of choosing the smallest element.

custom comparators for a struct

```
struct Car {
        float power;
        float weight;
};

bool compare_weight (const Car& a, const Car& b) {
        return a.weight < b.weight;
}

bool compare_power (const Car& a, const Car& b) {
        return a.power < b.power;
}
```

Almost every STL algorithm also comes with a version where you can provide a function that customises its action. In the case of `min_element()`:

customising algorithm

```
Car cars[] = { {100.f, 1300.f}, {90.f, 1200.f}, ... };
int sz = sizeof(cars)/sizeof(Car);

Car *lightest = min_element(cars, cars+sz, compare_weight);

cout << "lightest car has weight: " << lightest->weight;
```

> The *comparators*, as used by STL algorithms should take two arguments, and return a `bool`. The return value should be `true` if first argument is *less* than the second argument.
>
> **typical form of a comparison function**
>
> ```
> bool compare (T first, T second) {
>         if (first<second) return true;    // strictly less
>         return false;                     // otherwise
> }
> ```

A short list of algorithms that use *compare functions* are:

- `min_element()`, `max_element()`, `minmax_element()`
- `sort()`, `stable_sort()`, `merge()`
- `lower_bound()`, `upper_bound()`, `equal_range()`
- `set_union()`, `set_intersection()`, `set_difference()`
- `binary_search()`

5.2 Customising algorithms with predicates

Predicates define a condition under which an action takes place or not.

count_if() uses a predicate

```
bool is_even (int x) {
        return (x % 2) == 0;
}

vector<int> v = { 1, 2, 3, 4, 5, 6 };

cout << "number of even numbers in container is: "
     << count_if(v.begin(), v.end(), is_even);
```

There are a number of functions that require a predicate. They are easily distinguished by the *if* in their name:

- find_if(), find_if_not(), count_if()
- copy_if(), remove_if(), replace_if()
- partition()
- all_of(), any_of(), none_of()

5.3 Copying algorithms

You can copy from between any container type, using the same algorithm family – std::copy():

basic use of std::copy()

```
int source[9] = { 1, 2, 3, 4, 5, 6, 7, 8, 9 };
vector<int> dest;

dest.resize(9);
copy (source, source+9, dest);      // replace
```

This is a low-level way of using copy(), since it requires that the memory for destination container has already been allocated/reserved.

You can use the same algorithms in order to append, prepend, or insert into a container.

5.3.1 appending

The following use of copy does not require that the destination is pre-allocated.

use `back_inserter` on `copy()` to call `push_back()`

```
int source[9] = { 1, 2, 3, 4, 5, 6, 7, 8, 9 };
vector<int> dest;  // = { 20, 30, 40 }

dest.resize(9);
copy (source, source+9, back_inserter(dest));   // append

// dest is: { 20, 30, 40, 1, 2, 3, 4, 5, 6, 7, 8, 9 }
```

When the back_inserter() is used, `push_back()` is used in every iteration, to append to the destination container.

5.3.2 prepending

use `front_inserter` on `copy()` to call `push_front()`

```
int source[9] = { 1, 2, 3, 4, 5, 6, 7, 8, 9 };
vector<int> dest;  // = { 20, 30, 40 }

copy (source, source+9, front_inserter(dest));   // prepend

// dest is: { 1, 2, 3, 4, 5, 6, 7, 8, 9, 20, 30, 40 }
```

When the front_inserter() is used, `push_front()` is used in every iteration.

5.3.3 inserting

use `inserter` on `copy()` to call `insert()`

```
int source[9] = { 1, 2, 3, 4, 5, 6, 7, 8, 9 };
vector<int> dest;  // = { 20, 30, 40 }

copy (source, source+9, inserter(dest, dest.begin()+2));   // insert at index 2

// dest is: { 20, 30, 1, 2, 3, 4, 5, 6, 7, 8, 9, 40 }
```

When the inserter() is used, `insert()` is called on every iteration, to copy to the destination container. Notice that you state the *position* where you want the insertion to take place. For std::set, which is an ordered container, the position you insert at plays no role for the result [1] – simply set it to dest.begin().

---

[1] for std::set and std::map, the insertion position is simply a *hint*, for quicker insertion.

5.3.4 transforming while copying

Copying data often involves changing their type, converting or transforming them.

use std::transform() instead of copy() to convert data

```
int invert (int x) {
        return -x;
}

int source[9] = { 1, 2, 3, 4, 5, 6, 7, 8, 9 };
vector<int> dest;   // store negative values here

transform (source, source+9,
           back_inserter(dest),
           invert);   // invert() before copying



// dest is: { 20, 30, 1, 2, 3, 4, 5, 6, 7, 8, 9, 40 }
```

5.4 How are algorithms implemented ?

5.4.1 std::min_element()

Here is a model implementation of `min_element()`. This version uses a *custom compare function*. Now that you know how *compare function* is accessed, you can guess its prototype. The prototype is the same for all *compare* functions in STL.

a model of std::min_element()

```
template <class Iter, class Compare>
  Iter min_element ( Iter first, Iter last, Compare comp)
{
  if (first==last) return last;
  Iter smallest = first;

  while (++first!=last)
    if (comp(*first,*smallest))
      smallest=first;
  return smallest;
}
```

5.4.2 std::find_if()

Here is a model of `find_if()`. It uses a *predicate function*. Notice its prototype. All predicates in STL have the same prototype. `find_if()` returns an iterator to the first element that satisfies the predicate, or the the `last`, if no elements satisfy the predicate.

a model of `std::find_if()`

```
template<class Iter, class Predicate>
Iter find_if (Iter first, Iter last, Predicate pred)
{
  while (first!=last) {
    if (pred(*first)) return first;
    ++first;
  }
  return last;
}
```

5.4.3 std::for_each()

`for_each()` is the simplest of all implementations. It requires a *unary function*[2] object to call.

a model of `std::for_each()`

```
template<class Iter, class Function>
Function for_each (Iter first, Iter last, Function func)
{
  while (first!=last) {
    func(*first);
    ++first;
  }
  return func;
}
```

Notice the object returned by `for_each()`. It returns the function object that we passed as an argument. This allows for usages like:

---

[2] a *unary function*, in STL nomenclature, is a function with a single argument.

using the return value of std::for_each()

```
struct accumulate {
        int value;

        accumulate()
                : value(0) {
        }
        void operator() (int x) {
                value += x;
        }
};

vector<int> v = { 1, 2, 3, 4, 5 };
int total = for_each(v.begin(), v.end(), accumulate()).value;
cout << "total is " << total;
```

> Even though function objects are passed by value, this does not cause a performance issue. This is because function objects are small, and only passed once to the algorithm, not on every iteration. Also, since function objects are passed by value, this ensures that they exist in the stack. Data that exist in the stack are always *in* the CPU cache. This allows for great performance.

5.4.4 std::copy()

copy() copies a range of data from one container to another. The container types need not be the same:

a model of std::copy()

```
template<class InpIter, class OutIter>
OutIter copy (InpIter first, InpIter last, OutIter result)
{
        while (first != last) {
                *result = *first;
                ++result;
                ++first;
        }
         return result;
}
```

copy() reads the contents of an *input iterator*[3] and writes it where the *output iterator*[4] points to.

5.4.5 std::transform()

transform() is similar to copy(), but puts the data-to-be copied through an *operator* first.

a model of std::transform()

```
template<class InpIter, class OutIter, class Function>
OutIter transform (InpIter first, InpIter last, OutIter result, Function op)
{
    while (first != last) {
        *result = op(*first);
        ++result;
        ++first;
    }
    return result;
}
```

5.5 What is the fastest way to learn STL algorithms ?

Although currently the list of algorithms in STL are more than 80, learning them is not that difficult because of their naming convention. I used cplusplus.com[5] which contains the list of all algorithms, along with clear model implementations and short examples. I spent 5 minutes each day to read through each one.

---

[3] *input iterator* is just a naming convention which denotes that the iterator should support *reading* from it, i.e.: value = *it;
[4] *output iterator* is just a naming convention which denotes that the iterator should support *writing* to it, i.e.: *it = value;
[5] http://www.cplusplus.com/reference/algorithm/

6 Callable Objects

Callable objects and algorithms go together like bread and butter. There are various ways to call an algorithm:

```
vector<int> v; // = { 5, 3, 4, 1, 2 }

for_each (v.begin(), v.end(), do_some_work);
```

Here, `do_some_work` is some *callable object*. There are 4 forms a callable object may have:

- a function pointer
- a function object
- a function wrapper created by `bind()`
- a lambda function

To appreciate how callable objects work with algorithms, let's see how the algorithm could be implemented[1]:

for_each() implementation

```
template <typename Iter, typename Fun>
void for_each (Iter first, Iter last, Fun func) {
        while (first != last)
                func (*first);
        ++first;
}
```

Here, `func` is a templated parameter type, which means that you are free to pass any type to it. In fact, the only rule that `func` should obey, is that you should be able to use it like `func(*first);`

This means that `func` could be a *function pointer*, and `first` could be a *pointer* or an *iterator* to some type.

6.1 Using functions as callable objects

Here's one example of what `func` could be:

---
[1]for comprehensive implementations of STL algorithms, visit http://www.cplusplus.com/reference/algorithm/for_each/

function as a callable object

```
void print_int (int num) {
        cout << "Number is " << num << endl;
}

// use with iterators
vector<int> v; // = { 5, 3, 4, 1, 2 }

for_each (v.begin(), v.end(), print_int);

// use with pointers
int array[] = { 5, 3, 4, 1, 2 };
int sz = sizeof(array)/sizeof(int);

for_each (array, array+sz, print_int);
```

This is a very straightforward way to call the algorithm. But very soon one realises that func has the restriction that it can have only one parameter, which is very limiting for practical use.

Ideally, you would like to have its parameter used on another object:

```
void write_int_to_file (int num, FILE *fp) {
        fprintf (fp, "%d ", num);
}
```

Next, we study how this is done.

6.2 Using function objects as callable objects

In C++ you can make a struct imitate a function call. In order to achieve this, you need to provide the struct with operator().

the essentials of a function object

```cpp
struct WriteInt {
        void operator() (int num) {      // the function
                cout << "Number is " << num << endl;
        }
};
```

To call this function, we have to create an object of type `WriteInt` first. Then you can call it with parentheses, with an `int` argument, like so:

```cpp
WriteInt obj;
obj(999);   // prints: "Number is 999"
```

Syntactically, it looks as if we're calling a function, but in effect we call the member function `operator()` of `struct WriteInt`.

We can use this similarity to function call like so:

passing the function object to the algorithm

```cpp
vector<int> v; // = { 5, 3, 4, 1, 2 }

WriteInt obj;
for_each (v.begin(), v.end(), obj);
```

To simplify code and make it more readable, we create a temporary object when calling `for_each`:

passing function object to the algorithm as a *temporary object*

```cpp
vector<int> v; // = { 5, 3, 4, 1, 2 }

for_each (v.begin(), v.end(), WriteInt());
```

What happened here is that we pass the object as a parameter to `for_each()`. In our case, `WriteInt` is an object of *zero size*. The object acts like a function, hence its name, *function object*[2]

This object is still plain, like function `write_int()`, in the previous example. Let's beef it up a bit:

---

[2] another name used in the literature for function object, is *functor*.

function object with data

```
struct write_int_to_file {
    FILE *fp;                      // data

    void operator() (int num) {    // the function
        fprintf (fp, "%d ", num);
    }
};
```

Now, this functor still takes one argument in its operator(), but it can finally do something meaningful on another object.

```
FILE *p_file = fopen("out.txt", "wt");

vector<int> v; // = { 5, 3, 4, 1, 2 }

write_int_to_file obj;
obj.fp = p_file;
for_each (v.begin(), v.end(), obj);

fclose(p_file);
```

Again, to make things more readable you can create a temporary object, by providing a *constructor* to the functor:

function object with data and constructor

```
struct write_int_to_file {
    FILE *fp;                      // data

    write_int_to_file(FILE *p) {   // constructor
        fp = p;
    }

    void operator() (int num) {    // the function
        fprintf (fp, "%d ", num);
    }
};
```

The constructor allows you to setup the function object in one step. You should use it as the entry point for all the data the functor needs.

readable version of a function object with constructor

```
FILE *p_file = fopen("out.txt", "wt");

vector<int> v; // = { 5, 3, 4, 1, 2 }
for_each (v.begin(), v.end(), write_int_to_file(p_file));

fclose(p_file);
```

You can extend this concept by adding more pointers to the struct.

 The only thing that is necessary for a functor is an operator(). However, if the functor structure contains data, you should provide a constructor. This will enhance readability.

Hint:

To change the value of a variable, the functor should hold a *pointer* or a *reference* to this value. For example, to accumulate the entries of a vector, store a pointer to sum:

```
struct add_to {
        int *sum;

        add_to(int *p) {
                sum = p;
        }

        void operator() (int num) {
                *sum += num;
        }
};

vector<int> v; // = { 5, 3, 4, 1, 2 }

int total = 0;
for_each (v.begin(), v.end(), add_to(&total));
```

 Notice that the functor names that I'm picking are such, so that the algorithm reads like English.

6.3 Using `std::bind()` to create callable objects

6.3.1 Rationale

Sometimes there are library functions which are well known, but calling them via a functor obscures them.

Consider the following example:

function object calling `strcpy()`

```
struct copy_string {
    char *dest;

    copy_string(char *str_dest) {
        dest = str_dest;
    }

    void operator() (const char *src) {
        strcpy(dest, src);
    }
};
```

`strcpy()` is not a function to be called lightly, because it might write on memory that it does not have access. Callers should always be aware that they use it.

function object hides the fact that `strcpy()` is used

```
char sentence[1000] = "";
char* words[] = { "Hello", "World", "again" };

for_each (words, words+3, copy_string(sentence));
```

Although the functor in code above does its best to express its intention by choosing a good name, the reader of the client code would benefit if it was transparent that it is `strcpy()` that is actually doing the work. This is because callers usually know the dangers and limitations of `strcpy()`, and they would like to be aware of its presence.

For cases like that, it is better to use `std::bind()`:

bind() makes it transparent that strcpy() is used

```
char sentence[1000] = "";
char* words[] = { "Hello", "World", "again" };

for_each (words, words+3,
          bind(strcpy, sentence, _1) );
```

What does std::bind() do ?

bind(strcpy, sentence, _1)); calls strcpy(sentence, *ith-word*);

bind() creates an adaptor between the algorithm's call and the destination function. Although for_each() makes a call to func(char *str), bind redirects func to strcpy and the parameter, str, to _1.

bind(strcpy, sentence, _1) means:

- call strcpy(),
- with sentence as first argument, and
- _1 as the second argument, where _1 corresponds to the first parameter of the call to func().

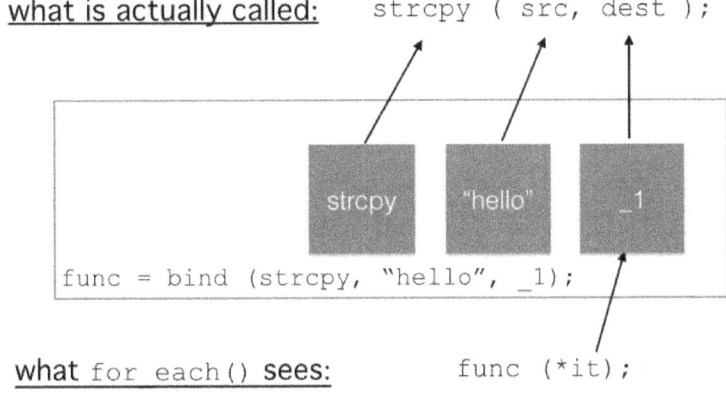

std::bind() creates a function object that rewires the parameters to a function

equivalent sequence of for_each(words, words+3, bind(strcpy, sentence, _1));

```
strcpy(sentence, words);
strcpy(sentence, words+1);
strcpy(sentence, words+2);
```

 Note that the complete way to call it is:

```
std::for_each (words, words+3,
               std::bind(strcpy, sentence, std::placeholders::_1));
```

The advantage of bind is that it adapt the algorithm's call to almost any function prototype. bind takes any number of parameters, like so:

bind(*[function]*, *[1st_function_arg]*, *[2nd_function_arg]*, *[3rd_function_arg]*, ...)

where any of the arguments can be a placeholder (_1, _2, etc).

The chapter 'std::bind() by example' contains extensive examples for you to get acquainted with its syntax.

However you put it, std::bind adds a lot of noise and twist to the way you read code. But it was the only tool in C++03 for composing function objects automatically. That is until *lamda functions* were possible in C++11.

6.4 Lambda functions as callable objects

From C++11 onwards, there is an extra tool for creating function objects.

Lambda functions are essentially *unnamed function objects*.

Lambda functions are a language feature, unlike std::bind, which is a library tool. This implies better syntax, performance, debugging and compiler error report.

We can rewrite the previous example like so:

calling algorithms using *lambda function*

```
char sentence[1000] = "";
char* words[] = { "Hello", "World", "again" };

for_each (words, words+3,
          [=] (const char *w) {
              strcpy(sentence, w);
          }
```

Despite its awkward syntax at first site, lambda functions are very useful when you want to compose functions without inventing names, or moving logic away from the eyes of the reader. The code inside the lambda function is plain code, without any special syntax rules. Hence it reads nicely.

The '[=]' in the first line denotes that a lambda function starts. The (const char* w) is the function prototype. Notice that it matches the function prototype that for_each() requires from its functions.

The scope of this book is only introductory, so I will not delve much into lambda functions. You'd need a C++11 course first, and I think that Stroustrup's book[3] does a good job on this field.

6.5 When to use each type callable functions:

The strategy you use to choose between choosing callable object, depends on the C++ compiler you can use:

- C++03 with tr1
- C++11

6.5.1 strategy on C++03 compiler

- **function pointer**
    Use this method if you have a function that plugs perfectly to the algorithm's call prototype.
    Note that, in this case, the algorithm makes the calls via function pointer, which may add an unnecessary dereference.
- **function object**
    Function objects are best when performance is critical. Function objects allow the optimiser to inline the call to operator() inside the algorithm.
    Function objects promote readability to algorithm calls. By giving suitable name to the function object, the algorithm call can read like English.
    Function objects can have data members. Which means they can have *state*. This can give you great flexibility when making repeated calls to it.

---

[3] http://www.stroustrup.com/4th.html

- bind

    Use bind when it is important that the internals of the callable object must not be hidden away.

    Use bind when you only need to adapt the interface of the algorithm call to the target function's prototype.

    Objects created by bind do not have state.

    Calls to the function adapted by bind involve two successive calls to function pointers. Therefore avoid bind when performance at that point is critical.

6.5.2 strategy on C++11 compiler

- function pointer

    Use this method if you have a function that plugs perfectly to the algorithm's call prototype.

    Note that, in this case, the algorithm makes the calls via function pointer, which may add an unnecessary dereference.

- function object

    Function object is essentially a *lambda function with name*.

    If the function needs to be reusable, write a function object.

    Given a suitable name, function objects can make the call to algorithm read like English.

    Function objects may have member functions. When setting up a function, or requesting results from it, is a task that requires many steps, use a function object.

- lambda function

    Use lambda function when you do *not* want to hide the internals of the function.

    When finding a name for a function object is difficult, a lambda function may be more appropriate option.

- bind

    you almost never need to use it. It is practically deprecated[4] by lambda functions

6.6 std::bind by example

std::bind creates a function object that stores a function, and some arguments for the function call.
std::function can store function objects, and call them when needed.

Let's assume you want to adapt calls to foo():

---

[4]just like std::bind1st() and std::bind2nd()

foo prototype

```
void foo (int a, int b, int c);
```

You can set up a call to foo() using bind() and call it at a later time:

making a function object that will call foo(arg1,arg2,arg3);

```
int arg1, arg2, arg3;

// function object's prototype
std::function <void ()> fun_obj;

// store the function object
fun_obj = std::bind (foo, arg1, arg2, arg3);

// call the function object
fun_obj();  // calls: foo (arg1, arg2, arg3);
```

using std::placeholders you can allow function object arguments to be passed on to the adapted function:

making a function object that will call foo(arg1,arg2,var);

```
std::function <void (int)> fun_obj;

fun_obj = std::bind (foo, arg1, arg2, std::placeholders::_1);

fun_obj(222);  // calls: foo (arg1, arg2, 222);
```

- std::placeholders::_1 redirects the 1st argument of the function object to the adapted function.
- std::placeholders::_2 redirects the 2nd argument of the function object to the adapted function,
- and so on

using many placeholders

```
std::function <void (int, int)> fun_obj;

fun_obj = std::bind (foo, std::placeholders::_2, arg2, std::placeholders::_1);

fun_obj(222, 333);   // calls: foo (333, arg2, 222);
```

`std::bind` can be nested:

nested calls to bind

```
std::function <void (int)> fun_obj;

fun_obj = std::bind (foo,
                     std::bind (boo,
                                std::placeholders::_1),
                     arg2,
                     std::placeholders::_1);

fun_obj(222);   // calls: foo (boo(222), arg2, 222);
```

`std::bind` can call member functions of classes:

class prototype

```
class Object {
    void member(int);
};
```

To call a class' member function, you need to get the pointer to that member function.

using bind to pass arguments to a member function

```
Object *obj = new Object();

std::function <void (int)> fun_obj;

fun_obj = std::bind (&Object::member,
                     obj,
                     std::placeholders::_1));

fun_obj(222);   // calls: obj->member(222);
```

The object itself can be an argument of the function object, by setting the placeholder to the appropriate position.

using bind to call a member function on a variable object

```
Object *obj = new Object();

std::function <void (Object *)> fun_obj;

fun_obj = std::bind (&Object::member,
                    std::placeholders::_1,
                    arg1));

fun_obj(obj);   // calls: obj->member(arg1);
```

Beware, that bind copies all of its arguments, therefore the following will not work as expected:

bind arguments are held by copy

```
void increment (int &n) {
    n++;
}

int count = 0; // variable to be incremented

std::function <void ()> fun_obj;

fun_obj = std::bind (increment,
                    count);   // a copy of 'count' is passed

fun_obj();   // count==0 -- oops!
```

To tell bind that you want count to be *passed by reference*, use std::ref():

using std::ref() to hold arguments are by reference

```
fun_obj = std::bind (increment,
                    std::ref(count));   // 'count' is passed by ref

fun_obj();   // count==1 -- correct!
```

Consequently, large object are not passed by reference, they are copied, so be careful:

bind arguments are held by copy

```
void print (const string &s) {
    cout << s;
}

string large_string = "a_very_large_string";

std::function <void ()> fun_obj;

fun_obj = std::bind (print,
                large_string);   // copies the string

fun_obj();
```

To successfully pass the argument *by const reference*, use

using std::cref() to hold arguments are by const reference

```
string large_string = "a_very_large_string";

fun_obj = std::bind (print,
                std::cref(large_string));   // pass by const ref

fun_obj();
```

Of course std::ref() would have worked here, equally well.

6.6.1 Summary

> **calling a function**
>
> bind (foo, arg1, arg2, arg3) will call foo (arg1, arg2, arg3)
>
> bind is formed like: cA> : bind(*[function], [1st_function_arg], [2nd_function_arg], [3rd_function_arg], ...*)
>
> **where any of the arguments:**
> can be a *placeholder* (_1, _2, etc), or
>
> may be passed by reference, using std::ref(), or std::cref()

calling a member function

bind (&MyClass::function, obj, arg1, arg2) will call obj->function (arg1, arg2)

bind is formed like:
    bind(*[member_function]*, *[the_object]*, *[1st_mem_func_arg]*, *[2nd_mem_func_arg]*, ...)

where any of the arguments:
    can be a *placeholder* (_1, _2, etc), or

    may be passed by reference, using std::ref(), or std::cref()

7 Avoid using low-level strings

C-style strings require too much housekeeping. Code is susceptible to bugs and memory leaks.

7.1 Problem description

You do not know when a function returns a pointer to a string, or to a copy of the string. You simply cannot trust the return value of a function.

Consider the following code, that uses a function, change_working_directory().

```
const char *old_dir;
const char *new_dir;

change_working_directory ("~/books/literature");
old_dir = get_working_directory();

change_working_directory ("~/books/comics");
new_dir = get_working_directory();
...
```

What is the string for old_dir and new_dir ?

It should be that old_dir is "~/books/literature" and new_dir is "~/books/comics". But it actually depends on the implementation of get_working_directory().

typically, you can get the current working directory using this method.

```
int sz = A_FILENAME_MAX;
char *cwd = malloc(sz);
if( !getcwd( cwd, sz ) ) {
    if (errno == ERANGE) {
        do {
            sz *= 2;
            cwd = realloc(cwd, sz);
        } while (getcwd(cwd, sz) == NULL && errno == ERANGE);
    }
    else {
    }
}
```

If get_working_directory() is implemented as:

```
const char* get_working_directory()
{
    int sz = A_FILENAME_MAX;
    static char *cwd = malloc(sz);    // static, to avoid allocations
    ...
    return cwd;
}
```

then old_dir and new_dir will be the same, namely "~/books/comics". Which is *totally counter intuitive*!

If this is the way that get_working_directory() is implemented, you would have to write

```
const char *old_dir;
const char *new_dir;

change_working_directory ("~/books/literature");
old_dir = strdup (get_working_directory());

change_working_directory ("~/books/comics");
new_dir = strdup(get_working_directory());

...
free(new_dir);
free(old_dir);
```

We have guarded ourselves from unexpected behavior, taking a big hit in readability.

Unfortunately, this is not a global solution against this type of problems: the code now runs the risk of *memory leaks*.

What if get_working_directory() is implemented like this?

```
const char* get_working_directory()
{
    int sz = A_FILENAME_MAX;
    char *cwd = malloc(sz);    // non-static
    ...
    return cwd;
}
```

In this case, it is the *user* who is responsible of freeing the string.

```
const char *old_dir;
const char *new_dir;

change_working_directory ("~/books/literature");
old_dir = get_working_directory();

change_working_directory ("~/books/comics");
new_dir = get_working_directory();

...

free (new_dir);
free (old_dir);
```

As you can see, there's no way you can compose the user code to guard against any kind of implementation of such functions. Even if one looks at the declaration of the function, he cannot tell whether he owns the string returned, or not.

7.2 The solution

The solution is to use C++'s string. In this case, we can implement get_working_directory() was so that it returns a string:

```
string get_working_directory()
{
    int sz = A_FILENAME_MAX;
    char *cwd = malloc(sz);
    ...
    return string(cwd);
}
```

This leads to a user code which is always safe, and easy to read.

```
change_working_directory ("~/books/literature");
string old_dir = get_working_directory();

change_working_directory ("~/books/comics");
string new_dir = get_working_directory();

...
```

now, this code

- is easy to read
- requires no housekeeping (no calls to `free()` are needed)
- the strings returned *can* be changed - they are *not* const
- there are no surprises when it comes to calling `get_working_directory()`

8 Understanding cache issues

Classical algorithm analysis is dominated by $\mathcal{O}$ notation. Modern CPUs are quite more complex than they used to be. It is therefore necessary to have a better picture of the issues that affect speed of execution.

Modern algorithm analysis does not rely solely on $\mathcal{O}$ notation. There is a different cost between arithmetic operations and operations that involve memory access.

Robert Sedgewick[1], in his online classes[2], suggests that we ought to count how many memory accesses and arithmetic operations an algorithm takes, in order to predict its execution time.

Alexander Stepanov[3], designer of the STL, in his classes at Amazon[4], postulates a small, set of proxy classes to count such operations.

8.1 Running costs of a program

Arithmetic operations vary in execution time. An *addition* is faster than a *multiplication*, which is faster than a *square root* operation. The ratio of clock cycles between these operations is steady. You can only do this much to save up on a few operations.

Memory access operations are very critical in the overall performance of an algorithm. This is because the execution time of a single memory access can vary between 3 and 200 cycles. The cost of a single memory access doubles once you move from a DDR2 memory to DDR3. It doubles once more, when you move from DDR3 to DDR4, and so on. This means, that

 if you do not design your algorithm properly, it will run twice as slow in a few years, when the next generation of memory modules is introduced.

Think about it: on a newer and faster machine, the *same* code, with the *same* amount of data will run at *half* the speed, on the next generation of memory modules. Consider that in the future, the amount of data that your algorithm will be faced with is likely to increase, too. This should convince you to try to understand memory issues.

---

[1] http://en.wikipedia.org/wiki/Robert_Sedgewick_(computer_scientist)
[2] https://www.coursera.org/course/algs4partI
[3] http://en.wikipedia.org/wiki/Alexander_Stepanov
[4] in the 'Efficient Programming with Components' lecture series, on YouTube.

8.2 Data access costs

The CPU accounts for only 1% of your processor's area. About 85% of the processor's area is occupied by cache. The rest of the area is devoted to data fetching mechanisms.

The way the computations take place is:

- data are fetched from memory into cache,
- data is loaded from cache to registers in the CPU,
- CPU performs calculations between registers
- results are stored back to cache
- results are written back to memory

In effect, CPU only interacts with data in cache. When data requested is not in the cache yet, the instruction halts until data is fetched from memory into cache.

The reason why cache is needed is to perform something like impedance matching. Data existing in cache takes about 3 cycles to reach a CPU register. Data existing in a DDR memory module, takes about 200 cycles to reach the processor.

This is partly because of physics. Within the tick of a 1GHz clock, i.e. within 1 nano sec, the signal would not travel more than 30cm (1 foot). On a 5GHz processor, the speed of light would not be enough to get a signal from the memory to the processor within a cycle.

The 200-cycle delay though is really caused by the circuitry design. Each megabyte requires some chip area. As storage requirements grow, you need more chip area. Although transistors get smaller, the growth in storage requirements is greater. So engineers need a way of saving up chip area. To achieve that, they simplify control circuitry.

There are now less control transistors per megabyte of storage than there used to be some years ago. So, now, whenever you request for a byte at a particular address, the DDR will send you a whole packet of consecutive data. With this concept, the data rate (bandwidth) is increased. But more signalling is required to tell memory which packet is needed. Therefore latency is increased.

 You can now get a whole packet of data with one request, but the pack of data will arrive much later.

This explains the trend in memory-module design:

- *bandwidth* will double on every new chip generation, and
- *latency* will also double on every generation

This implies that large chunks of consecutive data are faster to process, but sparse data will be much slower to process.

Large packets of consecutive data are fetched from memory into cache. As long as your program accesses data in this packet, data access will cost less (∼3 cycles for data in level 1 cache, ∼10-20 cycles for data in higher level cache). Once you try to access data that does not reside in cache[5], the execution halts until data is fetched to cache. Every cache miss therefore costs about 200 cycles.

Data does not always wait in the cache for you. It is limited in size (typically 8MB), so whenever new data needs to enter the cache, some data will leave.

access data from	time cost
level-1 cache	∼3 cycles
level-2 cache	∼10 cycles
DDR2 memory	∼200 cycles

8.3 Costs depending on data structures

A tree structure is likely to have its nodes scattered all around the memory area, depending when each node was allocated. This means, that apart from the $log(N)$ accesses needed to find a particular node in a tree, each access is likely to cost 200 cycles.

On the contrary, a binary search in an array is less likely to hit a cache-miss. All the data are likely to live in the same packet.

Even if you decide to create the tree in a memory pool[6], it can be up to 5 times more likely to incur a cache miss, compared to a vector. This is because each node of a red-black tree contains an overhead of at least 5 pointers, effectively inflating and scattering your data.

An array, on the other hand is a very compact data structure, on a contiguous piece of memory. These properties are very cache friendly.

Cache friendly data structures can run faster by up to two orders of magnitude. Therefore, $\mathcal{O}(N^2)$ algorithms are likely to run faster on a vector than an $\mathcal{O}(log(N))$ algorithm on another data structure.

This is why Stroustup advocates that you should always default to using a vector, even if other data structures promise a better performance, based on the big Oh notation.

8.4 Instruction Pipeline

Modern CPUs can execute multiple independent instructions in the same cycle, in the same core. There are architectures that the instruction contains 5 to 30 stages. This means that:

---

[5]this is widely known as a *cache miss*

[6]by *memory pool*, I mean a contiguously allocated memory, devoted to storing data for a special purpose, in this case for storing nodes of a particular tree.

```
int r = (a+b) * (c+d) * (e+f) * (g+h);
```

can be executed as

cycle	instr. stage 1	instr. stage 2	instr. stage 3	instr. stage 4
1	r1 = a + b	r2 = c + d	r3 = e + f	r4 = g + h
2	r5 = r1 * r2		r6 = r3 * r4	
3	r = r5 * r6			

instead of a linear execution

cycle	instruction
1	r1 = a + b
2	r2 = c + d
3	r3 = e + f
4	r4 = g + h
5	r5 = r1 * r2
6	r6 = r3 * r4
7	r = r5 * r6

The compiler can find *independent instructions* and execute them simultaneously. This works well only if there are many independent instructions. But there's not enough freedom for such trickery in a small loop like this:

```
for (int i=beg; i<end; i++) {
   a[i] = a[i] + 33;
}
```

In cases like this, the compiler unrolls the loop and lays the instructions in a pipeline[7].

In the older days, one would have to unroll the loop like that to give the compiler a chance to pack more instructions in a cycle:

---

[7] http://en.wikipedia.org/wiki/Instruction_pipeline

unrolling the loop

```
for (int i=beg; i+3<end; i+=4) {   // 4-stage loop
    a[i+0] = a[i+0] + 33;
    a[i+1] = a[i+1] + 33;
    a[i+2] = a[i+2] + 33;
    a[i+3] = a[i+3] + 33;
}
if (i+2<end) {                      // 3-stage remainder
    a[i+0] = a[i+0] + 33;
    a[i+1] = a[i+1] + 33;
    a[i+2] = a[i+2] + 33;
    i+=3;
}
if (i+1<end) {                      // 2-stage remainder
    a[i+0] = a[i+0] + 33;
    a[i+1] = a[i+1] + 33;
    i+=2;
}
if (i<end) {                        // 1-stage remainder
    a[i+0] = a[i+0] + 33;
    i+=1;
}
```

The loop would be laid out in one independent row of instructions per stage. The following table shows the pattern used to achieve that. Of course, the actual assembly code varies from architecture to architecture[8], but this is the main idea:

cycle	instr. stage 1	instr. stage 2	instr. stage 3	instr. stage 4
1	r1 = a[i]			
2	r1 = r1 + 33	r2 = a[i+1]		
3	a[i] = r1	r2 = r2 + 33	r3 = a[i+2]	
4		a[i+1] = r2	r3 = r3 + 33	r4 = a[i+3]
5			a[i+2] = r3	r4 = r4 + 33
6				a[i+4] = r4

The number of independent steps varies with the machine architecture. Intel Pentium 4 can have 7 up to 20-stage pipelines. As you can guess, this can easily give you a x10 increase in speed, for loops.

But this is not easy to achieve for any loop that the compiler might encounter. If the loop encounters a branch, it might have to throw away data that have been calculated:

[8]for a more detailed implementation of pipelining, watch 'Execution Cycle of the AVR Architecture', by Abelardo Pardo (University of Sidney), in YouTube

code with branches might break the pipeline

```
for (int i=beg; i<end; i++) {
   if (a[i] > 100)
      a[i] = a[i] + 33;
   else
      a[i] = a[i] + 44;
}
```

This means, that if you branch often, you will lose the x10 speed increase. Also, pipelining does not really apply when you have to access data of, say, a tree. This is because all the instructions will have to wait the memory accesses of a pointer, that contains a pointer, that contains a pointer ... until you reach the actual data. It is practically impossible to unroll code like that.

if you want to maximise speed[9]

- don't store data unnecessarily	cache is limited
- keep data compact, and	use a vector
- access memory in a predictable manner.	pay attention to branches

In effect, this is possible to occur on arrays and `vector`s, and up to some extent on `deque`s. Therefore, a `vector` can gain an extra increase in speed due to pipelining. This, combined with the speed gains you get because of the limited cache misses, makes Stroustrup say[10] that

the `vector` can be up to 3 orders of magnitude faster than a binary search tree, when it comes to linear operations. Therefore `vector` should be the default choice of container.

8.5 Side-stories

Here are a couple of examples of what gains you can get if you optimise for cache.

8.5.1 Rewriting an algorithm for GPU

I have often considered using the GPU to speed up execution of an algorithm. I then modified the implementation of the algorithm, so that it can be parallelised:

- remove function pointers,

---

[9] This wording is taken from: https://isocpp.org/blog/2014/06/stroustrup-lists
[10] Watch "Lists are Evil", part from Stroustrup's talk in GoingNative 2012, in youtube.

- remove conditionals from loops,
- place data in arrays instead of trees.

And then I discovered that the code suddenly runs so much faster on the CPU, that there is not going to have much impact if you rewrite it for GPU! This is to demonstrate the extent to which you can increase execution speed if you lay out data in a better manner.

If you follow the advice in how to maximise speed, your program is more likely to run faster in every next generation memory modules. If you don't, it will run slower!

8.5.2 De-virtualisation and Data Layout

This story is from a project at Facebook[11], presented by Andrei Alexndrescu. They have been trying to optimise code in order to use level-1 cache more. They rewrote their JIT compiler, in order to speed it up. Every 1% improvement in the JIT compiler's speed translated to many years of an engineer's salary, in power costs alone.

Andrei points out that **data layout is really important**. In fact, the first 64 bytes of a struct should contain the most commonly needed data. This is related to the fact that level-1 cache lines are typically 64-bytes long.

Andrei's rule of thumb for efficient cache usage:

variables in the struct (member variables) should be sorted by frequency of use:

- most used variables should be at the top of the struct, and
- less frequently used variables should be at the bottom.

This also lead to the consideration that they should try to *de-virtualise* some classes. Polymorphic objects contain a pointer to virtual-table in the first position – per base class, that is. This is not a very frequently used piece of data in time-critical algorithms. Therefore, they devised methods to removing polymorphisms from such objects.

This story demonstrates how power costs can be achieved by making efficient use of cache.

---

[11] http://channel9.msdn.com/Events/GoingNative/2013/Writing-Quick-Code-in-Cpp-Quickly

9 Converting a .c module into a .cpp

C++ is almost 100% compatible to C code. But in general you can't just rename a .c file into a .cpp and expect it to compile. You have to follow three steps to make the code compatible.

Let's consider what needs to be done to convert a C file and its respective header, into C++. Here is a typical situation, starting with a file.c and a file.h:

Header: `file.h`

```c
#ifndef FILE_H_INCLUDED            // include guards
#define FILE_H_INCLUDED

#include "point.h"                 // included files

struct Line;                       // forward declarations

void output_point (void *data);    // function declarations
struct Line* make_line (struct Point p1, struct Point p2);

#endif  /* FILE_H_INCLUDED */
```

"file.c"

```c
#include "file.h"

void output_point (void *data) {
        struct Point *pt = data;
        printf("[%.1f, %.1f, %.1f]\n", pt->x, pt->y, pt->z);
}

static int is_valid_point (struct Point *pt) {
        ...
}

struct Line* make_line (struct Point p1, struct Point p2) {
        struct Line *line = malloc(sizeof(struct Line));
```

```
        ...
}
```

There are a few steps you need to take, so that your project compiles when you convert `file.c` into `file.cpp`

9.1 Ensure header is readable by C++

After functions are compiled, the linker kicks in, to link function calls to the functions themselves. For this to take place, a linker needs to be able to refer to a function. The linker uses a symbol table for that. Each function has a symbolic name (a string, composed mainly of its function name, but not only) and a place where the body of the function can be found. The composition of the symbolic name (also known as name-mangling[1]) is different between C and C++.

Therefore, the compiler will create different symbol names for a function, depending on whether it was compiled using C or C++. A C program cannot call C++ functions. But we can tell the compiler to make a C++ function look like a C function. We simply need to tell the compiler to make a symbolic link using the C name-mangling. The way to do this is to define and declare it as:

```
extern "C" void foo(void *);
```

or, alternatively, for many functions

```
extern "C" {
        void foo(void *);
        void boo(int   );
        void goo(float );
}
```

but in C, the declaration should look like

```
extern void foo(void *);
extern void boo(int   );
extern void goo(float );
```

To do this collectively for our header, we use the `__cplusplus` definition, which exists only when the module that's being compiled is a .cpp. Note that any included files are outside the `extern "C"` scope.

---

[1] http://en.wikipedia.org/wiki/Name%5Fmangling

file.h

```c
#ifndef FILE_H_INCLUDED                    // include guards
#define FILE_H_INCLUDED

#include "point.h"                         // included files

#ifdef __cplusplus
extern "C" {
#endif

        struct Line;                       // forward declarations

        void output_point (void *data);    // function declarations
        struct Line* make_line (struct Point p1, struct Point p2);

#ifdef __cplusplus
}
#endif

#endif  /* FILE_H_INCLUDED */
```

9.2 Mark external functions as extern "C"

Next step is to go into file.cpp and mark any extern functions as extern "C". There is no need to mark the static functions. Remember that this step is necessary *only* for extern functions that need to be callable from C, as well.

file.c

```c
#include "file.h"

extern "C"
void output_point (void *data) {
        ...
}

static int is_valid_point (struct Point *pt) {
        ...
```

```
        }

        extern "C"
        struct Line* make_line (struct Point p1, struct Point p2) {
                ...
        }
```

9.3 Replace implicit casts from void *

The generic `void*` is commonly used in C. In C++ any pointer can be implicitly converted to a `void*`, but not the opposite. To perform an explicit cast, use `static_cast`. You can also use the C-style cast but it is not recommended. Prefer the `static_cast` as it will guard you against unsafe conversions (such as `double` to `Point*`).

```
struct Point *pt = data;                          // C code - does not compile
struct Point *pt = (Point*) data;                 // C-style cast
struct Point *pt = static_cast<Point*> (data);    // static_cast -- prefer this
```

and don't forget

```
struct Line *line = malloc(sizeof(struct Line));                          // C code \
 - does not compile
struct Line *line = (Line*) malloc(sizeof(struct Line));                  // C-style\
 cast
struct Line *line = static_cast<Line*> (malloc(sizeof(struct Line)));  // static_\
cast -- prefer this
```

9.4 Replace <math.h> with <cmath>

You may experience some advantage if you use the C++'s equivalent headers instead of C. For instance, `abs(real_value)` is the source of many bugs, as it silently clips any floating point value to int. In contrast, `std::abs(real_value)` does not bear any surprises. check the `abs()`, `fabs()`, `pow()`.

10 References

Books

1. *The C++ Programming Language*, 4th Edition by Bjarne Stroustrup
2. *Lean Architecture: for Agile Software Development* by James O. Coplien and Gertrud Bjornvig
3. *Clean Code: A Handbook of Agile Software Craftsmanship* by Robert C. Martin
4. *Effective STL: 50 Specific Ways to Improve Your Use of the Standard Template Library* by Scott Meyers

Conference Talks

1. *DCI: Re-thinking the foundations of object orientation and of programming*, by Trygve Reenskaug, at 0redev
2. *C++11 Style*, by Bjanrne Stroustup, at GoingNative 2012
3. *C++ Seasoning*, by Sean Parent, at GoingNative 2013
4. *Compiler++*, by Jim Radigan, at GoingNative 2013
5. *Writing Quick Code in C++, Quickly*, by Andrei Alexandrescu, at GoingNative 2013

Video Lectures

1. *Efficient Programming with Components*, by Alexander Stepanov, at YouTube
2. *Algorithms, Part I*, by Robert Sedgewick, at coursera.org
3. *Execution Cycle of the AVR Architecture*, by Abelardo Pardo, at YouTube

Web Pages

1. **Learning STL algorithms**:
    http://www.cplusplus.com/reference/
2. **Supporting blog for various issues of this book**:
    http://cpp-tip-of-the-day.blogspot.gr
3. **GoingNative conference talks**:
    http://channel9.msdn.com/Events/GoingNative/
4. **On Branch Prediction**:
    http://stackoverflow.com/questions/11227809/why-is-processing-a-sorted-array-faster-than-an-unsorted-array

5. *non-copyable* objects
   http://stackoverflow.com/questions/2173746/how-do-i-make-this-c-object-non-copyable
6. **Copy-On-Write**:
   http://stackoverflow.com/questions/12199710/legality-of-cow-stdstring-implementation-in-c11
7. **deleting elements of an STL map while iterating**:
   http://stackoverflow.com/questions/4600567/how-can-i-delete-elements-of-a-stdmap-with-an-iterator
8. **Rules for cache-friendly code**:
   https://isocpp.org/blog/2014/06/stroustrup-lists
9. **Google C++ Style Guide**:
   http://google-styleguide.googlecode.com/svn/trunk/cppguide.xml

www.ingramcontent.com/pod-product-compliance
Lightning Source LLC
Chambersburg PA
CBHW080930170526
45158CB00008B/2230